INFLUENCE

HOW TO EXERT IT

INFLUENCE

HOW TO EXERT IT

Yoritomo Tashi

Updated by Arthur R. Pell, Ph.D.

ANTHEM

An Imprint of Manjul Books

First published in India by Anthem,
an imprint of:

MANJUL BOOKS

Manjul Books Pvt. Ltd.
10, Nishat Colony, Bhopal - 462 003 INDIA
Phone : 91-755-4240340, Fax : 91-755-2736919
E-mail : manjul@manjulindia.com
Website : www.manjulindia.com

First published - 2006

Cover & book design by Manjul Creative Team

ISBN - 81 - 89631 - 05 - 5

Printed & bound in India by
Thomson Press (India) Ltd. Faridabad, INDIA

Dr. Arthur R. Pell holds B.A., M.A. and Ph.D. degrees and a professional diploma in Personnel Psychology and is a renowned author, lecturer and consultant in human resources management. He has worked with companies, government agencies, universities and non-profit organizations in the areas of employment, training, employee counselling, motivation and communication.

Dr. Pell is the author of numerous articles, audiocassette training programmes and 50 books on management, personnel, career planning and human relations, including *The Supervisor's Infobank: 1000 Quick Answers to Your Toughest Problems* and *The Complete Idiot's Guide to Managing People*, which has sold over 125,000 copies. He is a frequent commentator on radio and television and has conducted seminars and workshops on various aspects of human resources management that have been attended by over 250,000 people throughout the United States and Canada.

CONTENTS

FOREWORD TO ORIGINAL EDITION:

Yoritomo-Tashi, whose precepts are presented in this book, ranks as one of the three greatest statesmen that Japan has ever produced. He was her most illustrious and wise Shogun, and, as founder of the first Japanese dynasty of Shoguns, the reviser of the Empire's code of laws, and the organizer of military feudalism, he rescued his native land from the slough of demoralization into which it had sunk. In 1186, he established the seat of his government at Kamakura, where he organized an administrative body, similar in its methods and operation, to the metropolitan government. From what is known of his public career, it is evident that the great Shogun exercised a dominant influence over the minds of his people. To him, the art of influencing others was the key to Success. The great philosopher believed that the spirit of the individual continuously exerts influence, even as the flower also exerts influence by spreading its fragrance in the air. But just as the blossom cannot tell whither its fragrance spreads, so none of us can say how far our influence may reach. To an anonymous writer, we owe the thought that "Influence never dies." Every act, emotion, look, and word make it felt for good or evil, happiness or misery.

In the twelve lessons that Mr. B. Dangennes has drawn from the writings of Yoritomo-Tashi, and has presented in this book, the manner in which Influence may be exerted and the means by which it may be exercised, are considered. One lesson is devoted to the increase and expansion of psychic forces to awaken the dormant energies within us; another explains how influence may be exerted by persuasion and suggestion; a third shows the value of the fixed idea when supported by logical arguments; a fourth treats of the magnetic influence of the human eye and provides exercises for its development;

a fifth deals with the power of good example; a sixth points to value of perseverance - the achievement of great things by the utilization of spare moments; a seventh emphasizes the power of concentration and provides exercises for its acquisition, and an eighth shows that by exchanging confidence one may exert a mighty influence that can benefit even those suffering from mental and physical ailments. "Confidence," says Yoritomo, "is the foundation of courage and the mainspring of action." How much our own Emerson believed in this aphorism, he has told us - "Trust people and they will be true to you; treat them greatly and they will show themselves great." To confide in another, even though one may be betrayed, is better than to conceal. Those who suspect evil are seeking in their neighbor the very thing that they see in themselves, while those who exert useful influence are people of strength and initiative who consecrate their energies to the achievement of that which is good.

Throughout the following pages the editor has provided suggestions, examples, and exercises as aids to the reader in the acquisition of this, the desirable art of knowing how to influence others in the world at large.

Introduction by the Editor of the Original Edition

The success that has attended the publication of "Timidity Overcome," an earlier work by Yoritomo-Tashi, has encouraged me to print the precepts he developed on his methods of exerting influence.

The public can learn much from the old Shogun, whose doctrine, ringing with truth, is as applicable to the needs of our own days, as in the time when it was first revealed.

Moreover, it is embellished with legends, gentle or austere, which suggest the sight of a smooth, grassy slope on which appear, here and there, scattered among rough oak trees, the rarest and most exquisite flowers.

Thus, it is with a deep and serious joy, that I have again opened the manuscripts, to transcribe in our own beautiful language, the precepts and reflections of him who was at once a leader of men and a spiritual guide.

Again, little by little, I feel myself swayed by the charm already experienced; and the influence of these words, which seem to spring from the very beginning of time, and to have been diffused throughout the world, attract me and enthrall me with the doctrines of his philosophy in ever-increasing admiration.

Influence! that almost magical word, what things it suggests! To influence others! What a marvelous gift, and what assured success to those of us that possess it!

We will know only by name, the torments born of antipathy and of the loneliness of self-isolation from the rest of humankind.

The weaknesses of the will, the terrors that cause the rise of the phantom of agonizing doubt, will be strangers to us. Both the spirit and the body will be under our command.

The griefs of life never will completely overwhelm us, for, having foreseen them, we will know how to mitigate them.

We will have the joy of seeing that people's hearts, under the influence of our word and example, will open to pure and noble sentiments.

The art of succeeding will become familiar to us, for we will know how to attract to ourselves voluntary collaborators.

In short, our power will set us apart as a being different from others, and, to use an ancient Japanese saying, filled with dominating power: "We will build our palaces on the bones of the timorous."

Little by little, the radiating action of this expanding will acts on me; why not try, through Yoritomo, to speak of this art, more magnificent than all others, since it renders contagious the cult of proselytism and shows us how to prevent it from becoming sterile

To influence others! Is it not to play the part of creator, since it brings to life in all of our minds, an idea, which, without its aid never would have germinated?

Is it not to become a sort of providence, since good influence buries vice, the source of unhappiness and restlessness, to install instead perfect calm, the joy of living, and the security which always precedes happiness, or at least allows us to maintain ourselves in that state which most nearly approaches it.

With fervor, then, I have once more unfolded the writings of the philosopher, to transcribe the maxims and the luminous legends that make the study of his work so special and so attractive.

Although all truth is eternal, I trust that in this book, as in others that have preceded it, the reader will feel the undeniable and peculiarly genial attraction of the doctrine which the ancient Shogun exercises over the minds of those that know how to grasp and comprehend it.

B. Dangennes

Introduction to the Current Edition

Why republish a book that was written close to one hundred years ago and based on the writings of a Japanese shogun who lived in the 12th century?

Sure, some of the concepts Yoritomo-Tashi promulgated may seem alien to the sophisticated minds of the 21st century, but his basic philosophy, is to a great degree, pertinent today.

B. Dangennes, a French editor and writer recognized this when he came across Yoritomo's writings in the early 20th century. He was impressed with his deep insight into the human soul and his direct style and brilliance in defining the various states of the soul. Unlike so many other philosophers - both in the past and currently - Yoritomo is neither prosaic nor depressing. Neither is he satisfied with merely pointing out an evil. Instead, he analyses its causes and suggests practical solutions.

In addition to this treatise on influence, Dangennes edited two other works by Yoritomo: Common Sense: How to Exercise it and Timidity: How to Overcome it.

The purpose of this updated revision is to clarify and strengthen the book without tampering with the content. To make Yoritomo's message more accessible to the modern reader, we have changed some of the language to replace archaic terminology and some of the examples that he used.

Just reading a book on influencing others, will not help you become a more effective leader, unless you apply what the author recommends. You may not agree with or be able to apply everything Yoritomo suggests, but many of his ideas can be put into practice today, with the same effect, as when used by the shogun in his lifetime.

Arthur R. Pell. Ph.D.

LESSON I

By the Increase and Spread of Psychic Forces

"There is a country situated not far from the River Yet-Sin," said Yoritomo, "wherein certain villages are renowned for the curative property of the air."

"With the lightest breezes are diffused, balsamic odors, which pour into weak lungs, the restoring breath they pant for. At the coming of spring, invalids gather there to install themselves temporarily in tiny houses which, seen from a distance, look like huge birds resting for an instant before retaking flight."

"My venerated master, Lang-Ho, took me one day to visit this privileged country, and, while admiring the beauty of the landscape, I could not refrain from actions that showed clearly my surprise."

"In the gardens that surround the small houses, I see blooming, the amaryllis, opening its gorgeous chalices, from which spring pollen laden pistils, looking like a woman's long eyelashes that have been made heavy with paint; in the flower-beds bloom roses, delicate or pronounced in odor; while large convolvuli climb the roofs and fall in jagged clusters."

"The fields extend monotonously in the distance; strips of land were planted with solid banks of chrysanthemums, whose bitter odor we could plainly detect."

"But above all other odors rose the balsamic fragrance of the resinous trees, vivifying and persistent. Yet, though I looked around carefully, I could perceive no sign of these trees, whose odor filled our lungs."

"Then my master looked at me and smiled:

'I thought that you would be surprised,' said he; 'that is the common experience of those that visit this country for the first time; but how few among them are wise enough to draw a lesson from what they observed.' "

"Pointing at a low hill, whose silvery verdure appeared to stand out like a luminous mass against a sky of tenderest blue, he continued:

'Look! Behind that light screen of bushes is a grove composed of resinous trees. We cannot see them, but their beneficent influence diffuses itself throughout the surrounding country.' "

"Do not neglect the lesson this teaches, my son! That little grove of regenerative power happily, illustrates those people, whose influence radiates upon and extends itself over those that approach them, in pouring out upon them the balm it distils."

"Just as the light and frivolous birches hide the rough branches and roots whence proceed health and life, the art of influencing must learn how to surround itself with an aspect of amiability, and, in order to reach people's souls, it must abandon the idea that it must be composed merely of the rougher and more rugged virtues, so much extolled by many philosophers."

"Influence must know how to enter the most thoughtless spirit, after the manner in which the balsamic odor penetrates these petty little houses, with their gardens filled with useless flowers."

"Most invalids recoil at the mere notion of the boredom of living in the woods; but they come with pleasure to establish themselves among flowers, and yield unconsciously to the restoring influence, that radiates around them in the vivifying balsamic atoms."

"With the coming winter they will depart. They will take up their old way of life, detaching themselves completely from that which has given them a new birth, so to speak; but they will bear within themselves this principle of new life, which has implanted itself without their will, and which will by slow degrees develop itself in the form of a desire to return."

"Be not blind, my son, but receive seriously the lesson given to you by the immensity and simplicity of Nature."

"As she influences the body, know that she influences souls also; and your earthly sojourn should contribute to the instruction of a strong and supple race, whose power will assert itself throughout the centuries."

"People never really die who know how to assume sufficient empire over others to be able to trace lasting marks of their energy and power over the minds of those who, under their influence, bend their steps toward the highest."

"While he discoursed," Yoritomo continued, "I glanced around mechanically, and saw some of the inhabitants of these little pleasure houses. Some among them occupied themselves with light tasks of horticulture; others strolled about, chatting; the women, whom one could discern among the shadows of the terraces, were preparing tea with a cheerful rattle of cups; no one appeared to give a thought to the neighboring grove, yet every one felt its beneficent influence."

"An imperious and passionate desire arose within me to allow the expansion of the forces which energy, always working and always increasing, had put in my brain, that their powerful rays might penetrate weak souls and temper them for the bitter struggle of existence, by reawakening in them a resolution toward good and a hatred of evil, simultaneously with the dauntless courage which is the keynote of all success based on noble ambitions."

A single word struck me in this last phrase of the

Japanese philosopher.

He did not say, "to create," but to "reawaken" in people's souls, a resolution toward good and a hatred of evil.

It is this theory that our modern psychologists support so strongly; the plurality of types, which one may see verified in a single individual.

It is only in the simplest romances and the most naïve plays that individuals are good or bad all in the same way, without any variation.

On the contrary, it is easy to show that each individual is a prey, at a given moment, or in special circumstances, to contrary impulses, which show in him or her, the presence of a double sensibility.

We will not speak of inclinations which correct themselves or grow weaker after reflection; for example, the sudden and unlooked - for prodigality of misers who fancy they may gain something by a show of liberality; the voluntary self-indulgence of people who know how prejudicial to them may be an appearance of excessive strictness or severity; or the temporary abstemiousness of gourmands, who reserve their appetites for a feast.

Instinct, more often, takes the place of reason, in imposing on each person, acts of contradictory sentiment, according to the time, the place, or the circumstances.

Our mind is only too often the field of evolution, wherein, are elaborated resolutions that are not dictated by an attentive and conscientious will.

Our modern way of speech calls such persons impulsive; following the bent of the idea that haunts them, they may be heroic or cowardly, proud or servile, kind or cruel; it is often impossible for the observer, as well as for themselves, to determine the exact quality, whether good or bad, that plays the chief part in the character of the normal person.

"There are those," Yoritomo continues, "who, dazzled by the fantastic dreams of a theoretic existence, recoil before the effort necessary to re-establish themselves in actual life and in stripping the rags of illusion from their chimera."

"All those, again, whom inertia holds ensnared in their vices will feel their hearts moved by an emotion leading toward light, and toward the practice of virtues indispensable to him, who desires to face triumphantly, the conflict of existence."

Note that the Shogun does not speak of "creating" the feeling that gives the impulse toward good; he wishes simply to awaken it, for he knows that it dwells within every heart.

If it does not manifest itself, it is because the psychic qualities necessary to its production cannot create successfully the initial impulse, which, fortified by the will and rendered more precise by concentration, will become efficacious in forming a habit.

But, in order to possess this gift in a way complete enough to exercise its beneficent influence over others, that it may be possible to suggest favorable thoughts and draw us back from the incline of baleful resolutions, it is indispensable that we should provide ourselves with that beneficent power which must radiate from ourselves, as heat rises from a glowing hearth.

What must one do to gain this power?

Listen again to the Shogun.

"We possess," said he, "innumerable forces that lie hidden within ourselves, though it would be easy to lead them, as the waters of a canal are conducted, to make them serve for the conquest of good, spiritual as well as corporeal."

"The existence of these forces can not be doubted; they abide in a latent state in some persons, and appear intermittently in others."

"It is the lack of domestication of these forces that causes the frequent and disconcerting plurality of the Ego."

"What can one think of people who today commit villainous crimes and who to-morrow, in the same circumstances, will perform acts of devotion?"

"Thinkers have often deduced from this phenomenon

the theory that in such people slumber different states of the soul, of which one, under the influence of a momentary emotion, surges up, to the exclusion of all others."

"These manifestations of the energies that are buried in the most profound depths of being, are, unless they are concerned in our moral betterment, almost always regrettable because they are thoughtless, springing up incomplete and nearly always contrary to those designs, which deliberate reason would help us to accomplish."

"It is wise to direct these efforts to a practical end, and not toward such realizations of which the accomplishment would give no virile satisfaction."

Apropos of this, Yoritomo related the following little legend:

"Once on a time lived a man who was in love with the queen of the clouds."

"His days were passed in contemplation of the skies; when the sun shone he was sad, but when clouds floated across the heavens like gray tatters lie he delighted himself with fancying that he could behold his chimera."

"She was very capricious, and rarely assumed the same aspect twice. But from time to time, he recognized her in some flocculent mass, whereupon, his heart would swell with joy."

"At last, he resolved to join her, and in order to do so, he fancied he must build a monumental stairway that would reach to the sky. So he set himself to work, interrupting himself only to lose himself in the contemplation of his ideal."

"Years passed; his hair grew gray, his hands and knees trembled, but, faithful at his task, he continued painfully to add one step to another."

"At last a day came when the tottering builder, struggling in anguish against approaching death, attained his object; the stairway reached the clouds, from the midst of which his beloved leaned toward him."

"He climbed the last step and extended his lips to the longed-for apparition."

"But he received only the kiss of the rain which, dropping slowly, bore with it the form on which he had doted so many years."

"Returning to earth, the man wept."

"He wept for his lost youth, the beautiful years that had gone, and, above all, for his strength wasted in sterile efforts, when he might have put it to magnificent use."

May not this little legend be the origin of the story from which our modern writers have drawn the figure of Pierrot, the classic French clown, enamored of the moon?

Are there not many persons who pass their lives in building by slow stages, a stairway that leads nowhere, and who do not perceive the fact until the work is finished?

The struggle for life becomes more and more arduous, and the power of our hidden faculties should expand in accordance with ever-growing necessities.

It is time, then, to awaken the forces that lie dormant within us.

"But," some one may object at this appeal, "evil forces as well as good will be aroused, and the combat between them will be so much the stronger because we ourselves must direct it."

The old Japanese philosopher had foreseen this objection, and he said quietly:

"Why fear to reanimate all the possibilities that lie dormant in our natures?"

"Is it not desirable to cultivate all plants indiscriminately?"

"There are those that are poisonous, true, yet even these are indispensable in the practice of medicine."

"Large doses of certain drugs cause death; but, administered wisely with the hand of a skillful physician, they bring relief and very often a complete cure."

"The same may be said of many forces that are evil only because they are not disciplined."

"There is still a danger to avoid; that of failing to discern those, who can make us mistake for virtues, the evil qualities that are only deceptive copies of virtues."

"Just as certain poisonous vegetables resemble those that are edible and wholesome, just as certain flowers have the form and color of those that are inoffensive, up to the point where only the initiated can detect the difference, there are failings, which, by their origin, resemble virtues of which they are really the direct opposite."

"But naturalists are not deceived; the poisonous plant is recognized by them in the midst of a hundred others, and if they gather it, it is only to extract its medicinal properties."

Philosophers, adept in researches touching suggestion, distinguish still more rapidly the "enemy" forces that disguise themselves under an appearance of false virtue.

"They will separate pride from vanity, perseverance from obstinacy, gentleness from weakness; and, strong, in this knowledge, they will know how to gather and to infuse into weak souls the infinitesimal dose necessary to produce the auxiliaries to success."

I observed that this word "success" occurred frequently in the remarks of the Japanese philosopher.

It was because it is the "Open Sesame" of the magic gates that lead to the domain so much desired.

Success! It is the fulfillment of one or of several desires, all converging toward one end.

It is the reason for living for those who wish to struggle for the conquest of Good - that Good which has a way of transforming itself and seems farther away as soon as one has grasped it.

For wise people know the inanity of the word "perfection;" perfection cannot exist, since it cannot be absolute and is always debatable, following the bent of differing tastes or the application of doctrines.

A thing, that seems to some persons the highest degree of good, will be criticized by others, whose convictions modify the ideal.

At this point Yoritomo, as he delighted to do, illustrated his words with a fable:

"A man once lived," said he, "who resolved to climb to the highest summit of a chain of mountains, so that no obstacle should hide from him the view of the universe."

"After countless fatigues, he climbed the peak which from below seemed to him higher than all the others; the ascent was rough, the road arduous and dangerous; but the man, possessed by his idea, felt neither the scorching sun which burned his face, nor the biting north wind on wintry nights."

"In order to avoid precipices and possible traps along the road, he walked with bent head, and did not raise it until the moment when his feet reached the lofty plateau, the object of his strenuous efforts."

"Alas! what disillusion was his! A granite wall, which clouds had heretofore hidden from his gaze, on looking up from below, rose before him, straight, rigid, impracticable, as it seemed to him."

"Impracticable? Not entirely so, but perilous, and above all mysterious, for the clouds that enveloped it hardly permitted him to discern the road that he must follow amid a thousand dangers."

"The man postponed the accomplishment of his desire. He descended into the valley again to wait for the dispersion of the clouds, so that he could choose his road by a clearer light."

"But that was not the real cause of his chagrin. The topmost peak was invisible from below, and he asked himself bitterly whether his great fatigue had not been caused by a mirage, after all."

"Should he begin another ascent? It was such hard work - it was better to wait! Now that he knew from which side he should climb to reach the summit, there was no need to worry about it. Besides, did a summit really exist? And even if it did, might he not encounter, after a weary climb, still another eminence, which he had not yet been able to discern?"

"Days passed; the propitious moment did not present itself, and at last the man died in the valley, having lived a life interwoven with regrets and aspirations, the more cruel because he well knew that he had not the energy sufficient to satisfy them."

"This often happens to those that assign to themselves nothing short of perfection as the end of their efforts."

"As soon as they imagine they have attained it, they try sadly to ascertain whether there is not something more left to conquer."

"Those among them who have become wise compel themselves simply to attain the highest, and soon acquire a passionate enthusiasm for their task, for their aim is not circumscribed but grand and infinite."

"One should pity those who believe themselves to have 'arrived' quite as much as those who despair of arriving. The former, thinking they have nothing more to combat, soon come to believe that there is nothing more worth conquering."

"Combat increases our energies, and the desire to live becomes more determined when one fears that one must die before the task has been accomplished."

"But," asked some one, "when should we enjoy the benefits of our continued efforts?"

The answer was ready:

"From the perpetual pursuit of the highest springs a series of realizations, each of which gives us the joy and pride of conquest. Do traders cease to do business because they have just made a good bargain? While they appreciate the advantages gained in the long-pursued transaction, they will enter upon another into which they will throw themselves eagerly, and will even use the gains of the preceding bargain to make sure of negotiating the second."

"Thus we should use acquired forces, the advantages gained over ourselves, in the realization of another ideal, which, once attained, will allow us to pursue another of a form more nearly perfect."

"Those of us in whom moral strength does not grow and increase, are very near decadence, and that means that we will enter on the road leading to shadows and death."

"Let us then turn resolutely toward the light; above all, let us increase our psychic forces, for they alone can give us that power that emanates from certain beings whose domination exercises itself beneficently over those that surround them."

"Just as when, in the heat of the sun, all grains and seeds sleeping in the earth's bosom sprout and rise in the form of plants to play their part in the universal fête of Nature, so under the power of influence always augmented and disciplined by noble deeds, the hearts of those near us will open to a desire for the best, conducive to the general aim of human kind - Happiness."

LESSON II

By Persuasion

How little we realize, what a large part persuasion plays in our life. Clergy, teachers, lawyers, business managers, salespeople, parents - all are trying to persuade, to influence, to win over others to their way of thinking, to their principles, to accept their ideas.

Some people are so tactful, so sunny, so bright, cheerful, and attractive that they never have to force or even request an entrance anywhere. The door is flung wide open and they are invited to enter, just as we invite beauty, loveliness and sunshine to enter our mind. Their very presence has a subtle influence and is soothing and pleasing. They know how to persuade almost without uttering a word.

"Persuasion," Yoritomo taught us, "clothes itself in two very different forms; one invades the soul like the invisible molecules of a soothing balm poured from a kindly hand, gently infiltrating itself throughout our systems, communicating to us its virtues."

"The other may be compared to the terrible wind of the African deserts."

"If, from the first hour, we feel its burning touch, we have not known how to avoid it; by shutting ourselves closely within our dwelling, every crevice and opening of which has been sealed, nothing can escape its attacks."

"The imperceptible sand drifts little by little into all

corners of the house, and even reaches all parts of the human body."

"However well protected we may be, it even penetrates closed lips and eyes, and soon this almost invisible thing dominates us and becomes our constant preoccupation."

"Evil persuasion is all the more dangerous because it knows how to clothe itself with the most attractive external attributes."

"That is what we meet in the guise of counselors whose words are always tempting, since they adopt the false appearance of solicitude."

"With earnest words and sympathetic smiles, these persons who almost always have nothing to do in life, try to spoil the lives of others, without having a suspicion of their unconscious crime."

"Usually these are the kind of persons that talk in apparent good faith about the freedom to live one's own life."

"They are those who seek the agreeable sensation of the moment, without giving a thought to the possible bitterness of tomorrow."

"They have to learn harsh lessons, for all that; often they are compelled to suffer for days and weeks in order to pay for one day of careless pleasure; but these days are either soon forgotten, or their lightness of character is such that they prefer to take the risk of drawing down on themselves serious troubles in the future than to make any effort in the present to avoid them."

Here Yoritomo, always ready with examples, related the following story:

"I once knew a young man, the son of one of my friends, who was afflicted with a certain lightness of judgment."

"He was not bad at heart, but his effeminacy and lack of strength of will made him an undesirable companion for such of his young friends, whose souls were not sufficiently tempered by the practice of a continual appeal to dominating forces."

"One day he was calling on one of his friends, whose father occupied an important place in the senate, and who sent his son to the house of one of his colleagues to learn the result of a discussion in which he had not been able to take part. Apropos of a very important question, on which a favored future or a disgrace depended, he wished to know what a night session of the senate had determined."

"On the way, the son of the senator confided his apprehensions to his frivolous friend."

"To this young man these weighty matters seemed unimportant and childish, and he dwelt much on the boredom it would be, to allow this matter to spoil an evening in which both friends had promised themselves much pleasure."

"His reply filled the senator's son with consternation; the night session had taken place, and the most important affairs had been discussed, and the absent senator had been attacked with great bitterness by his adversaries."

"But the friend said, 'Since the contretemps is sure to bring trouble and spoil the pleasure we were looking forward to, why risk this trouble? We can tell your father that the session did not take place, and that all is going well!' "

"The senator's son resisted; he would not dare lie to his father, he said. But his friend became more insinuating: 'It would not be a serious lie, and besides, one would have time to say that some one had misunderstood - in fact, are we quite sure that there had not been some misunderstanding?' "

"In order to vanquish his friend's last hesitations, the young gentleman pretended to recall the whole interview, analyzing its details and inventing others. Meantime, he said, they would say that several persons had stopped them and questioned them; was it not to one of these that they had replied?"

"He said so much in so persuasive a way that at last the senator's son deliberately told his father that the expected session had been postponed until the following day. Under the influence of this evil persuasion, he felt not the slightest remorse in telling this falsehood, and passed a delightful evening."

"But alas! the next day must have been terrible!"

"His father and his partisans could not be found at all in time to foil the scheme of his enemies; his disgrace was decided on, and the order to commit hara-kiri was sent to him."

"After he was dead, his effects were confiscated, and his son dragged out the miserable existence of the poor beings whom will and dignity do not console."

The old philosopher did not tell us whether the friend, the cause of all these disasters, sought to palliate them by coming to the aid of him, whom he had ruined by his detestable counsel.

But it is probable that, feeling in this affair as those feel who are conscious of their contemptible conduct, he looked on indifferently at the misfortunes chargeable solely to his own lightness of character.

It is, in fact, a common trait with those who are conscious of their own inability to make the least effort to experience a wicked sort of pleasure in observing the failure of others.

Another variety of the agents of bad persuasion are those persons we call pessimists, whom Yoritomo describes thus:

"One should flee those who are created with life which makes one think only of the stupor of death."

"Their souls are always in the state where one finds the body in the tomb; every effort seems useless to them, or rather, they prefer to make a show of that indifference which makes the gestures necessary to obtain the accomplishments they pretend to despise."

"Despise them, indeed? Do they not feel, rather a malicious joy in demoralizing others?"

"They like to consider humankind as fundamentally bad, and to declare that the slumber of the dead is the superior of all other pleasures."

"That is true only regarding those who, as we have said, pass through life as if they were already dead."

"They would be right, perhaps, if one heard only through pleasures of the gross, earthly joys of existence."

"But, for those that know how to see, the joy of living is in all things, and we can taste it, even in the midst of the greatest afflictions."

"Can the grief of mourning, cruel though it may be, prevent us from admiring the sunshine at the moment when it hangs the purple of the sunset in the sky before it sinks to sleep behind the quivering birch-trees?

"Can any grief, whatever it may be, prevent us from feeling a delicate emotion on hearing the sweet, strong voice of a boatman, whose song is lost in the distance when his light craft disappears in the golden mist of the great lakes."

"The joy of life throbs everywhere about us; it is in everything that surrounds us, and we should gather all our strength to cry out against those that preach pessimistic doctrine, for every life, sad though it may be, is worth living."

Do we not hear those that talk about the scourge of our day, neurasthenia - which often is only one of the commonest forms of egoism for those that are attacked by it - refuse not only to believe in the beautiful and the good, but they devote the last sparks of their fast-disappearing will to persuading others of the uselessness of everything.

Are they always sincere? Do they not do this in a sort of spite against those who are more expert in the art of living and who excite their envy by enjoying the blessings of life that their own moral weakness does not allow them to appreciate.

How much happier are those of whom Yoritomo says, "They accept joyfully the evil of living," and show it in their fervent adoration of everything that is beautiful and good.

"These," he added, "are the true priests of favorable

persuasion."

"They know by the authority of their own conviction, how to give courage again to the weak and faith to the incredulous."

"By the virtue of persuasion, they banish from the invalid, the pains which almost always hasten the apparition of imaginary sufferings."

"They know the right words to say to strengthen weak wills, and to give to those who suffer pain in reality, the courage to support the ills which sympathy and solicitude make lighter."

"They are, in short, true healers."

"The persuasion toward health is the best of panaceas, for no one denies the influence of moral qualities on physical health."

"I once knew a man who, under the influence to one fixed idea, was about to die."

"He imagined that, while drinking the water of a stagnant pool, he had swallowed a serpent, minute at first, but which growing larger inside of his body, caused internal ravages of which he felt himself likely soon to die."

"His friends had told me of his singular case, telling me how anxious they were at seeing this so-called invalid wasting away day by day."

"I was curious to visit him; I found a real invalid, looking very ill, with features sunken, and hardly able to drag himself about. Pressing his chest, he told us that the serpent was devouring him."

"His friends laughed at him and seemed to think that I would join them in their mirth, but I judged the moral evil too serious to try to soothe him by trying to reason with him."

"Persuasion alone, based on a real or an imaginary proof, with the aid of suggestion, could save the man."

"Instead of laughing with the others, I pretended to believe that he was really ill, and asked him to tell me his story, to which I listened with the deepest attention."

"To his great astonishment, I sympathized with him in his trouble, and spoke of one of my friends, a famous healer, who would be happy to interest himself in the invalid and to try to save him."

"Two days later I returned, actually bringing with me a physician whom I had told of this strange mania, and who had promised me his assistance, for it was indispensable to have near me some one who could speak authoritatively in order to impress the mind of the invalid."

"He examined the patient carefully, prescribed certain medicines, and withdrew, without giving any words of positive hope."

"Then began my part, that of a psychologist."

"I pretended that I would tell him the absolute truth, however brutal it might seem. The doctor had discovered beyond all doubt the presence of the serpent; he had tried certain medication. Would it succeed? He dared not affirm it."

"Several days passed, with alternating fear and hope, indications I noted carefully. Finally, one day the physician declared that he was about to make a decisive test, of which he had great hope of a favorable result."

"I had known so well how to be persuasive, and had understood so thoroughly how to surround the patient with the right occult influences, that he no longer rejected the idea of a possible cure; and when, after taking certain medicines that induced him to vomit freely, we showed him the serpent which he believed he had thrown up; our invalid found himself suddenly cured."

"After this, if he happened to feel again pain or discomfort of any kind, he attributed it to the ravages caused by the serpent, and, as the cause existed no more, the evil soon disappeared."

"This case shows that one of the conditions of succeeding in the art of persuading is not to batter rudely at convictions that one wishes to uproot."

"This hardly requires an explanation; in order to persuade some one, it is necessary to merit his or her sympathy; now, one never gains the sympathy of those whose opinions he or she does not share."

"Hence, in order to persuade successfully, one must banish suspicion and know how to listen."

"One must not forget the profound egotism that characterizes all imaginary invalids; they are so full of themselves that their ills seem to acquire high importance to them."

"They cannot admit then that the whole world is not interested in their aches and pains, and the importance they themselves attach to them is a subject of development for their malady."

"For, it is incontestable that all moral emotion has an immediate repercussion on the physical state."

"To be able to persuade patients that they are cured is, in most cases, to free them from their malady; it is always infinitely attenuated, since it is to spare them moral uneasiness, which exacerbates their bodily ills."

But Yoritomo did not stop here with instructing us in the benefits of persuasion; he extended his remarks to the unfortunates who are assailed by the doubt even of happiness, and he encouraged them with this parable:

"A young lord was passing one day along the highroad when the sedan chair, on which he was being carried, was struck so roughly that it was broken to pieces. He looked at the ruins a moment, then he ordered his bearers to go in search of a new one, and sat down by the roadside to wait for them to bring it."

"A poor man passing by stopped and talked with him about the accident."

" 'And what shall you do with these pieces?' he inquired."

" 'Why, nothing,' the rich man replied; 'I shall leave them where they are.' "

"Then will you allow me to take them?"

"Yes, since I. don't want them."

"The beggar then set himself to work; he readjusted the boards, washed the soiled spots on the hangings in the nearest brook, and did so much and so well that toward evening the sedan chair, although a little deteriorated, it is true, was solid and fit to use again."

"Just then the bearers returned. They had not been able to find anything but a chair so light and frail that, as soon as they tried it, they saw that it would not do."

"There the beggar intervened, and offered the chair he had just repaired."

"The young lord was glad to pay a large indemnity to have the use for several hours of a thing which in reality belonged to him."

"And that," adds the old philosopher, "is the experience of many persons who will not understand that a destroyed happiness may prove a kind of blessing, if one knows how to gather up the pieces."

"Instead of grieving over them and abandoning them by the wayside in order to wait for what may turn up, is it not better to do as the beggar did and to seek in the mishap, a security, which we should find it difficult to be sure of in the coordination of new events?"

"It is on such occasions as this that the power of influence comes into play."

"In order to persuade people that it is easier for them to work at the construction (or reconstruction) of the happiness that is near them, psychic power is more necessary than it is in drawing them into hypothetic adventures."

"The fascination of beginning over again has attractions for not a few people and how many more rely on luck which they almost defy!"

"When can they convince themselves that, for those who know the power of influence, which develops a steady will and a strong thought, luck is born chiefly of circumstances created by ourselves."

"Almost always, we are the architects of our own fortunes; it is in working at them without respite that we may model them, if not wholly according to our wish, at least in a way somewhat approaching it."

"It is by believing steadfastly that we shall attain the highest power, that we shall acquire the qualities that make us almost more than human, since they allow us to govern and subdue those by whom we are surrounded."

Might we not say that here Yoritomo presented the "superman" of Nietzsche, and do we not find in all those theories a commentary on the modern phrase of the power of mind over matter?

In what manner does this evolution produce itself and above all, by what means can one obtain these quasi-miracles?

How does one make this effort to attain the desired end, and what qualities, occult or material are necessary to develop to attain this magnificent ambition to conquer the minds of others?

You can learn to be a persuasive person.

While it is true that some people have more natural capacity than others, it is also true that most people can, by training, acquire the skills needed to succeed.

Let's look at the one job where persuasiveness is a major element - salesmanship. Even if you are not selling a product or a service, but are selling your ideas to other people, you must think of yourself as a salesperson.

Whether you are selling a product or selling your boss to accept your ideas or persuading others to change their minds about a political issue, the steps of persuasion are the same.

The first step is to get the other person's attention, otherwise nothing you say will even be listened to. This is absolutely necessary before you can persuade anybody to do what you want done.

You can get attention by commenting about something you know will be of interest to the person to whom you are talking. It is not necessary to speak of trivial or extraneous matters to attract that person's attention. A direct question or comment on the situation involved, is a good first step.

For example, if you wish to persuade colleagues to serve on a committee to evaluate a new piece of equipment, a comment about the frequent breakdown of current equipment would surely get their attention.

The next step is to get them to be thoroughly interested in your proposition. You must arouse their desire to embrace the idea you are proposing. Once this is accomplished, acceptance is almost certain. To do this you must appeal to their emotions - the heart rather than the head.

First, you must explore what the other persons really want. What is important to them? What turns them on? To do this, you must truly listen to what they say in answer to your questions. Listen carefully. Be prepared to pick up subtleties that can lead you to that person's real interest. Then by adapting your comments to fit into their desires, you are on the way to winning your point.

Persuasive power, the ability to win others over to our way of thinking, our way of looking at things, is not a simple quality. It is in reality made up of many admirable qualities, which have more to do with the heart than the head. It is the emotional traits of human nature, which enables one to win out in many instances where logical qualities would be of no avail.

The best and most successful teachers are not always the most learned, but those who get hold of the hearts of their pupils, whose kindness, personal interest, and sympathy qualities which, apart from scholarship, make the best teachers. These same qualities give all of us the basic ingredients of being persuasive people.

The best sales people are those who look out for their customer's interests and only try to sell them what is to their advantage to buy. They will not work off a large bill of goods upon them, which they know in their hearts they should not buy.

The ability to make others think as you do, is a tremendous power, and carries great responsibility. Remember that the people with whom you are dealing will be always on guard against any sort of deceit. They will be looking for evidences of insincerity. They have no intention of allowing themselves to be duped or lulled. Be sincere!. Remember that there is no substitute for sincerity in any field.

LESSON III

The Influence of the Eyes

Few persons escape the influence of the human eye. If its look is imperious, it subjugates; if it is tender, it moves; if it is sad, it penetrates the heart with melancholy.

But this influence cannot be real and strong, unless it is incited by the thought behind it, which maintains and fixes that look, in communicating to it the expression either terrible or favorable, persuasive or defiant, which alone can maintain the firmness and the perseverance of the active forces of our brain.

"Some persons," said Yoritomo, "possess naturally a fascinating eye; usually they are those who can maintain a steady gaze for a long time without blinking."

"But it is not sufficient to be able to throw a glance, the persistence of which sometimes causes a passing discomfort, which almost always tends toward the subjection of spirits of the weaker sort."

"This look should be the projection of a thought in which the fixed form is definite enough, so that its penetrative influence shall become efficacious."

"But," some one will say, "it is not always necessary to think, since several animals possess this power of fascination, like the snake, which holds a bird motionless under the power of its gaze, so that it never dreams of trying to use its wings to escape from its enemy."

"But if conscientious thought does not exist in the animal, it is nevertheless active in responding to instinct."

"In the brain of the serpent there is a blind but highly concentrated power that manifests itself by its eager desire to seize its prey, and this power, placed at the service of a forceful instinct, develops a compulsion that is sufficient to paralyze all desire to oppose it in the weakest creature."

But the serpent does not monopolize this privilege of fascination, if one may believe certain old French chronicles.

In the old book published by Rousseau in the seventeenth century, it is related that a toad shut up in a vase that he could not get out of, found it difficult to endure the fascination of the human eye; at first, in evident uneasiness, it tried to escape; then, when convinced that that was impossible, it would return to its former position and stare at the person in its turn, and ended by dying of the effect of this peculiar force.

Is it necessary to lend strength to this story by adding that one day a toad, stronger or more irritable than the others, riveted its eyes so long upon a man's eyes that he actually felt the influence of the creature and swooned under the implacable fixity of its gaze?

I do not believe that such experiences have been officially established, but it is none the less interesting to conclude that if under the sway of an instinctive thought, the eye of an animal can acquire a rare power, the human eye, when animated by an active and reasonable thought, may be an important agent of influence and of suggestion.

"In order to convince your adversary," said the Japanese philosopher, "you must look him or her straight in the eyes."

"But it would be very stupid and unskillful to employ this method without discretion."

"Some would see in it only insolence, and their irritation would prevent them from feeling the full influence of the gaze; others would feel a certain uneasiness which would cause them to turn the eyes away before having submitted entirely to the gazer's influence, and might prevent them from renewing an interview with a person that had impressed them so unpleasantly."

"The best way to begin the use of the eye in influencing is to talk of subjects that will not arouse suspicion in the interlocutor."

"We should present ourselves in an easy and quiet manner and listen without showing any signs of impatience to whatever objections the person may make; some of these may not be lacking in accuracy, and it would be unwise to combat them."

"It is unnecessary to add that the least hastiness, which would displace the point of concentration of the thought, would be injurious, and might work serious harm to the success that we seek."

"Too great excess of modesty should be avoided, for the transmission of thought - and consequently of influence - is worked at our cost."

"Timidity is always an obstacle to the influence of the eye, which should, at the very first interchange of glances, look straight and frankly into the eyes of the interlocutor, at the top of the bridge of the nose."

"The first conflict once over, we should turn away our eyes carelessly; and should especially avoid the eyes of our opponent in the first minutes of conversation, before our own eyes have gained any hold on that person; we should in some way fix our gaze without allowing our opponent's eyes to gain a hold over our own."

"In short, if we wish to influence another by our look, we must take the greatest care not to let that person suspect our design, which would immediately put him or her on the defensive and render all our efforts vain."

"I once knew a young man named Yon-Li," added Yoritomo, "who went to call on a nobleman with the intention of serving as a mediator between him and one of his friends."

"In strict truth, I should say that the object of this

proceeding was not wholly disinterested, since he wished to urge the nobleman to conclude a transaction that was injurious to his own interests."

"Besides, the friend had promised a round sum to Yon-Li if he should succeed in influencing this important personage to the point of accepting this solution."

"For a long time, the young man had practiced exercises in the development of psychic influence, and he believed that he had arrived at the point when one is sure of himself."

"He entered and immediately threw on the nobleman, a glance, which the other thought rather singular; he tried to surmise the cause of a look which became almost aggressive in its expression of determination to dominate him."

"The nobleman was a man of strong will, who had for a long time exercised his powers of penetration."

"He had no great difficulty in discovering the motive that actuated the young Yon-Li, and he conceived the idea of fighting him with his own weapons."

"Taking care to avoid looking into the pupils of his visitor's eyes, he fixed him in the way which we have described, concentrating his gaze at the top of the bridge of the nose and strongly centering his thought on the idea of domination."

"The young amateur was not prepared to meet an attack more powerful than his own; his bold assurance faltered a little; under the influence of that penetrating look he blinked, lowered his eyelids, and gently turned away."

"He was vanquished, and it was with hesitation that he made his request. It was not entertained or even listened to, and he had besides the embarrassment of confessing, despite himself, the indelicate step which he had been ready to undertake."

Yoritomo added:

"The influence of the eye is undeniable; it is occult power set in vibration by the force of the thought; it is the result of the action of the forces that surround us, combined with our own vital force."

"One should not use these forces by chance. It is well to use them, especially, as arms, offensive or defensive, in the great battle won by wisdom and a knowledge of human nature."

But just as when he instructed us in the acquiring of energy, as well as when he taught us how to overcome timidity, Yoritomo did not content himself with uttering precepts; he told us the methods, whereby, we might acquire the precious gifts that he extolled.

"In order to attain that authority of the eye which is one of the first conditions in the study of acquiring mental dominance," said Yoritomo, "certain exercises are necessary: For example, it is well to lay a stick of bamboo across a sheet of paper, and then seat oneself at a few steps distance and stare fixedly at the bamboo without allowing the eye to wander to the sheet of paper."

"One must use all his strength of will to avoid blinking."

"This exercise should begin with counting up to twenty, then to thirty, increasing the enumeration up to two hundred, which is enough."

"When one can perform this first exercise easily, it will be time to pass to another, a little more complicated."

"Having made a hole in the sheet of paper - taking great care to pierce it in such a way, as to have the edges of the opening neat and clean-cut, rivet your fixed gaze on this aperture one, two, three minutes, longer if possible."

"It is well also to place yourself in front of a bright, smooth surface, preferably polished tin - lacking one of silver or gold - and to seek in it the reflection of your own eyes."

"Plunge your gaze into the inmost depths of your eyes; from the beginning this will be a good exercise in compelling the gaze of others to yield to your own."

"In this situation, turn the head from right to left, then from left to right, without losing sight of the reflection of your eyes."

"This strengthens the muscles of the eyes, and gives one's glance firmness and the desired power."

"Avoid blinking the eyes and lowering the eyelids, and practice meeting firmly the gaze of others."

But all these exercises would be in vain, if during the time of this contemplation, you do not know how to concentrate your mind on a single subject.

How much influence could you exercise over others if you do not know first how to master yourself?

Singleness of thought is indispensable during the development of the use of the eye; if it seems too difficult to keep it fixed on a single point, it would be well to avail oneself of certain means of suggestion, like the following:

"First, count up to ten with the simple idea of doing it slowly, and to allow the same space of time to elapse between the uttering of each number."

"Secondly, run through the fingers, a string of about sixty beads, counting them in a low tone of voice, without losing sight of the point one has fixed on."

"You may count at first up to five or to ten; then increase the count, taking care to begin all over again if you find your attention has wandered, or that while pronouncing the numbers it has been diverted, if only for an instant, from the single thought that is the object of your purpose."

But this is not all; as soon as you have acquired the desired qualities in the cultivation of the power of the eye, you should begin to experiment with them, and regarding this, here is what our philosopher counsels us:

"When you have mastered the use of the eye, and have learned how to concentrate the mind, try the ascendancy of your visual power on some person in the midst of a crowd."

"First, choose some one whose face indicates a character weaker than your own, and fix your gaze in the back of that person's neck, with a single thought, which shall invade that person's mind, haunting him or her with a desire to turn around."

"If your influence is already sufficiently formed, at the end of a certain time you will see that person begin to fidget, then to move his or her head slightly, as if to shake off an importunate thought; finally, your subject's hand will move to the spot on which your gaze has been fixed, then, without realizing the reason, he or she will turn around."

"This experiment may be made on all sorts of subjects, and it will always succeed on condition that you know how to envelop your subject in an intense mental current, the action of which will combine itself with the power of your gaze."

"You can imagine, then, to what extent this faculty may be useful in the ordinary circumstances of life; it is the secret of those we call fascinating persons, whom no one can resist and who know how to obtain anything they desire by merely saying what pleasure it would give them to possess the desired object; for they know well that in concentrating the mind strongly on that for which they ask, the mind of their interlocutor, yielding to mental sway, abandons itself easily, especially if the domination of the eye increases this conviction by creating in that person a psychic state which compels submission to its power."

These precepts were those of that other tamer of spirits, Mohammad, who said:

"The effect of the human eye is indubitable. If there is anything in the world that can move more rapidly than fate, it is the glance of the eyes."

From this saying, strong superstitions have arisen, against which the Shogun puts us on our guard:

"One of the reasons," says he, " that militate in favor of the cultivation of the influential use of the eye is the necessity of getting the better of a certain kind of persons who pretend to have inherited occult power from magicians."

"People gifted with strong wills have nothing to fear from these shameless liars; but sensitive and impulsive people, who do not know how to assert themselves and dominate others, become easy prey; and the suggestions of these wretches will soon lead them to dissipate their fortunes in answering their stupid requests."

"Besides," Yoritomo added, "those that would wish to use their occult influence to compel others to commit a wrong action would be soon punished by the loss of this influence, which develops itself gently only when actuated by beneficent thought; while they retract and end by becoming annihilated when the uppermost thought is of the kind of which may be said:

'Evil thoughts about others are rods with which we ourselves shall one day be beaten.' "

LESSON IV

Through Clearness of Speech

The word is the most direct manifestation of the thought; hence it is one of the most important agents of Influence when it clothes itself with precision and clearness, indispensable in cooperating, in creating conviction in the minds of one's hearers.

Were not the burning words of Peter the Hermit, the sole cause of the rising of arms for the crusade to conquer the tomb of Jesus?

And was it not especially because that monk believed himself firmly to be moved by a divine will that he knew how to make his belief shared by thousands of men of all classes, poor or rich, who, under the influence of his words, all possessed only a single soul, impregnated with sentiments of heroic piety, which urged them to dye the sands of Palestine with their blood?

What arguments had this monk found? Only three words, but powerful words, when one considers the mentality and the peculiar religiosity of that epoch: "God wishes it!"

"God wishes it!" These words were the first to declare to the ignorant masses Peter's all powerful influence. In the eyes of the vulgar, this man who transmitted to them thus, the will of the Most High, assumed in their eyes the proportions of a divine messenger, a sort of prophet in communication with the Master of Masters, who deigned to dictate to him

His orders.

For others, it was to resume debates by an argument without reply; it was to excuse fatigues and privations, and an unknown death under a foreign sky. God wished it! How vain were all other speeches after these three words, which bowed all heads under the powerful breath of divine domination, as wheat bends under the tempestuous winds!

Yoritomo speaks as a true sage, then, when he says:

"Leaders of souls should not forget this one thing: Too great wealth of words is hostile to conviction."

And, alluding to a Japanese proverb, which is very similar to one of our own well-known proverbs, he added:

"If speech is like jade, silence is like a diamond."

"Speech is like a diamond when it is the vibrating form of the concrete thought and when it presents itself in a quiet way, rendering its suggestions familiar and clear by the way in which the orator knows how to present them."

"Prolific speech is the medium of powerful thought - of that thought of which we should be master and not slaves."

"Speech is the seed, good or ill-omened, which, sown in irresolute natures, may produce either nettles or wheat."

"This may be also the 'fixed idea' that is supposed to be implanted in every weak brain."

"Suppose some one should chance to say to people, who are endowed with the power of initiative, but with a wavering will: 'You will be good, because goodness is the supreme end of life,' if the order is accompanied by the dominating look of which we have spoken and pronounced in a tone that will impress, there is no doubt that these influences will produce such a radiation as, in spite of themselves, would make them feel that they are under the influence of good emanating from themselves to converge toward other people."

"This may seem very obscure at first, but the brevity and precision of order will implant themselves little by little in the brain, of which the passive forces, always submissive to confused influence, will at a certain moment determine the active forces to emerge from the background where up to then, they had lain hidden."

"But if one expresses this prophecy some day before being afflicted with moral weakness: 'You will be a criminal,' the idea, originally repelled with horror, ends by sowing in the brain, an idea first of the impossibility of the suggestion then, more frequently evoked, it becomes less monstrous. It commences with a smile of doubt, then it evolves to fear. By facing the eventuality of this prophesied crime, the specter which had been pursued so persistently,. a time will come, when carried away by anger or a violent passion this criminal act was committed. What previously would certainly have been rejected, was now replaced with a new idea which was perceived as the instrument predestined by fate."

"That is the reason why," added the Shogun, with infinite wisdom, "one cannot blame too much, such parents, as prophesy for their children terrible punishments for reprehensible acts which they can hardly help committing."

And he added:

"Those who, thinking to cure their children of faults more or less characteristic, repeat to them: 'You will die under the executioner's whip,' are sometimes the involuntary cause of this execution."

"To strengthen this idea of so lugubrious a fate for the little ones, they familiarize them with it, and dwell on its horrors."

"Then they compromise constantly their authority before their children, for they, seeing them the next day filled with kind feelings and expressing tenderness toward them, will not fail to regard lightly, the terrible menace with which they were threatened."

"It might happen that they were struck by it, and that would be likely to be unlucky for their future, for, once implant this idea in their brains, they will not fail to wonder at the serenity of their parents, who can admit the possibility of so terrible a fate and yet go on living peacefully with the menace of such a future for their child."

"In every way, the authority of the heads of the family will find itself lessened, and the seed sown in the heart of the child by the imprudent prophecy can not fail to produce bad fruit."

"It will be so much the more dangerous if it should be resumed in a few words, those incisive words that draw mental pictures which take root in the brain."

"Long lectures have only a repressing effect on the spirit."

"One's listeners, endowed with will and discernment, very soon give up trying, under the avalanche of words that fall on their ears with the monotony of flakes of snow, to distinguish truths that are uttered in the confused mass of verbiage."

"On the contrary, they force themselves to turn these thoughts from this wordy chaos, in which the confusion equals the monotony."

"As for others, the laxity of their attention does not permit them to follow the same idea very long, and, all effort being painful to them, they will not follow long the orator's intricate mazes of thought."

"But those that know how to present their thought in a few phrases, in a way that impresses itself on their listeners, may easily become leaders of the masses."

"The first quality of the speakers who would be convincing should be able to think deeply of what they wish to say."

"As soon as they know how to transform their thoughts into clear-cut images, the contours of which will not admit of any one's divining one line to be different from the line intended, they will be careful to project these thoughts into the minds of others under the form of lights and shades."

"We have already seen how the power of thought had the gift of influencing others, particularly, when this force is aided by the power of the eye; when these two ruling faculties are augmented by the power of spoken discourse, the listeners are conquered by the ideas that are presented to them."

"Those that will acquire these gifts will find that they can interest others and attach them to themselves; in a word they, can lead them by means of the influence that will assure them of mental empire over most of their contemporaries."

"It is necessary, also," the Shogun continued, "to base oneself on the theory that like attracts like, in the expansion of the sympathetic radiation which must converge towards great numbers to illumine the human soul."

"It has been remarkable with what facility people follow noble impulses, heroic appeals, and generous outbursts."

"Speakers would be culpable, then, should they count on the inferior mental quality of their auditors in order to descend to their level."

"This is the fault of too many speakers who like to court less noble sides of the popular spirit."

"They give as a reason - I would almost say an excuse - that to address them in this way, one is better listened to and more readily understood."

"This is a gross error. How many times have I uttered a noble thought in the midst of an assemblage of persons of mental mediocrity!"

"As this thought was always expressed in language - clear and exact, formed of words that all could comprehend, every time I have had the pleasure of seeing the multitude vibrate like a harp struck by an expert hand, and to feel for a moment that the souls of the roughest of peasants were elevated under the influence of my words which were adapted to the purest ideal."

"Is not this a kind of conquest for which those that devote themselves to the art of influencing should strive?"

"It is by speech that one develops emotion, generator of noble gestures and of generous realizations."

"Speech is the distributor of the thoughts that surround

us, of which the reiterated suggestions, after impregnating certain groups of cells in our brain, travel, by affinity, to haunt the same group of brain cells in other auditors."

"This is one reason why it is not well to dwell too long on the same subject, so that one can allow some rest to the weaker brains in an audience."

"Still, it is an undoubted fact that to jump from one subject to another, and to leave them only to attack them again, as is the custom of some speakers, is more fatiguing and less satisfactory, for minds wearied by this continual exercise end by ceasing to follow the flight of these fugitive thoughts; and, after waiting in vain for some repose in a discourse, they give up trying to follow the constant flight of a too soaring imagination."

"Another type to be dreaded are those devoted to idle chatter and gossip."

"One might, if he were greatly in earnest, correct them in this way: listen to their conversation, summarize it, and in ten minutes repeat to them all that it had taken them an hour to say; by 'all' one must understand merely the ideas and not the repetitions."

"But will they stand corrected? Will they not do as did a certain lord who, having seen his neighbor very ill, and having talked incessantly while visiting him, without letting the sick man get a word in edgewise, said, when leaving him:

'I will return to-morrow to learn how you are, for I fear I have tired you very much because I have done so much talking today.' "

"Conciseness and clearness in speaking is thus a great force in the work of influencing, which is a noble task for one who undertakes it seriously."

"Moderation must be among the qualities whose aim is to second the action by the word in order to direct the focus of attention toward the principal thought which, excluding all accessory thoughts, should be imposed on the minds of the auditors by the speakers that wish to extend influence over them."

"Discretion is equally indispensable in forming influence by speech."

"From indiscretion to lying, the step is short, and one should not forget this axiom that might well be written in characters of jade on leaves of purest gold:

'Lying is a homage which inferiority renders unconsciously to merit.' "

"Bands of precious metals should be hung on the walls of salons, replacing, in a way more comprehensible to all minds, the covered rose filled vases that ornament festal tables."

And Yoritomo reminded us of that ancient custom, which we believed peculiar to the Grecian sages, and which, it appears, was begun centuries ago among the philosophers of the Far East:

"Harpocrates, the god whom the ancient Greeks worshiped under the image of silence had presented to Eros, the God of Love a flower which, coming from his hands, represented the virtue which he was supposed to symbolize."

"This gift was made in order to encourage the wanton boy to guard the secrets of his mother Venus, for we know that Eros was always ready to reveal the secrets of those that were attacked by his flames."

"This act of the god was imitated first by the Grecian sages, then by the Japanese philosophers; and at all banquets appears a closed vase, the cover of which must not be lifted."

"This vase encloses the roses, whose perfume filters through the interstices of the vessel, letting one guess what flowers are within."

"It was a custom to ask the guests to let nothing transpire regarding the discussions that took place in these gatherings."

"Later the custom became general and was followed among ordinary people, when the closed and flower-filled vase was a constant warning to the guests to use discretion, and not to allow to escape outside anything that might have been said under the influence of wine."

"Our modern humor has immortalized this custom in the form of a figure of speech that is on everybody's tongue, but of which few persons know the origin: people often say of one who tells secrets: 'He has uncovered the rose jar!' "

The etymology of this figure is known to few, but, however that may be, we are grateful to Yoritomo for recalling it to us by connecting it with one of the lessons he has taught us, which, disguised in the form of a parable, fix them in our minds, in so attractive a fashion, that we do not forget them as soon as we have heard them.

LESSON V

By Setting Good Example

We read in a Japanese story that once man set out in pursuit of a rose. He sought it a long time, but nothing seemed to him to be that flower, which he knew only by hearsay, that praised its incomparable perfume and the beauty of its multiplex corolla.

"He saw the admirable amaryllis, balancing on flexible stems their odoriferous chalices, whose tender tints were touched with brown spots, that seemed like the tears of night."

"He had inhaled - quite surprised to find them without perfume - the breath of the proud peonies which bloomed near by, looking like a sort of burning bush."

"The fragrant stalactites of the acacias had breathed upon him their balmy odor."

"He had paused before carnations, which, crimson in their green chalices, looked like the throats of warriors, bursting out of their armor."

"The sumptuous mourning of the black lily also had attracted him; but none of these flowers were, nor could be, the rose, and he was almost in despair when he saw, quite near him, alight on a bush, a butterfly of the most dazzling colors, and a delightful aroma seemed to be diffused from it, while its wings quivered like the petals of a flower shaken in the wind."

"Greatly moved, the man approached it, saying:

'Beautiful creature, glowing with colors so brilliant and exhaling a perfume so sweet, can it be that you are the rose?' "

" 'No,' said the butterfly, 'I am not the rose, but I live near the rose; I love the refuge of her flowery arches and branches. I come to sleep in the hollows of her corollas, and sip the sweet perfume of her flowers.' "

"That is the reason why I have become so thoroughly impregnated with her odor as to deceive you."

This little fable may serve as a preface to anything one might say or write on the force of example.

Our most frequent associations are never indifferent to our mentality, and we always submit, voluntarily or unconsciously, to the ascendancy of those that surround us, unless we have sufficient influence over their minds to compel them to submit themselves to us.

Then the thought, projected into an enveloping center by a superior influence, is received by brains of weaker caliber, which register it mechanically, in order to reproduce it on similar occasions.

Our popular modern philosophy has put this maxim into a proverb:

"Tell me who are your associates and I will tell you what you are."

It is explained also by Baron Charles Du Potet, a nineteenth century exponent of magnetism, in his "Magnetic Therapeutics."

"There are certain persons," he said, "who when near you, seem to draw something from you, to pump you, to absorb your force and your life; a species of vampire, without knowing it, they live at your expense."

"When near them, in the sphere of their activity, one feels an uneasiness, a constraint which is caused by their pernicious actions and determines in us an indefinable feeling."

"You are moved by a desire to escape and to go far away from them; but these people have quite the opposite tendency; they come nearer and nearer to you, press close to you, seem fairly to wish to join themselves to you, to draw from you that which is necessary to their lives."

"Other persons, on the contrary, bear with them life and health."

"Wherever they go, they seem to radiate joy and sunshine."

"You observe that their conversation pleases and that people seek them out. One likes to touch their hands, to lean on their arm; something soothing which charms and magnetizes you, quite unconsciously, seems to emanate from them."

"One easily adopts their point of view on things in general, and their opinions, without knowing why; and one sees them go away with sincere regret."

In short, above all things regarding psychic influence, we must not forget that "the strongest reason is always the best."

Unfortunately, the strongest is not always that which is worth the most; a regrettable contagion follows from the person who suffers the ascendancy of the other.

"Or again," the old Shogun explained, "the reciprocal influence which individuals exercise on one another is the cause of many evils difficult to conjure."

"That, if we may believe tradition, is the reason why the sages of old created so-called mutual admiration societies, to which only those of undisputed merit were admitted."

"In the numerous reunions, whatever might be the apparent reason for them, a low mentality evinced itself, and the general quality of thought became inferior, to such a degree that the most elevated mind felt the difficulty of escaping the contagion of the surrounding mediocrity."

"The only influence of orators might be to transmute souls, momentarily, by substituting for mean and niggardly thoughts, a current of broad, generous ideas, from which would spring an enthusiasm real, but almost always ephemeral, for at the moment of realization, particular interests, narrow views, and the fear of responsibility will give back to each one of their auditors, the mind that belongs to him or her, which a profound study of the attainment of the highest and best alone could transform slowly and definitively."

"However, certain such circles do exist which are composed of persons of absolutely pure aspirations, all communicant toward a noble end, in a collective thought, the waves of which are voluntarily directed toward a single accomplishment."

From these reunions of the best minds, emanates a current of influence the value of which is considerable, since emulation, the offspring of example, is found in these circles where, each one developing, in a sense, from the same principle, concentrates his or her faculties on the search for the best in all that is good.

"But it is very difficult to maintain these gatherings under the unique direction of the original generous spirit. To find people who will ignore questions of temporary supremacy and of particular interests, and to know how to repress petty antipathies and hatreds, possibly more or less justifiable, in order to open the heart to the creation of an ideal - this is almost to expect the impossible."

"Is it, indeed, necessary to ask it? Is it well to suppress ambition in a person's heart? Does not such a leveling tend to destroy the seed of individual responsibility, a cognizance of which leads to the most noble conquests?"

While admiring the scruples of the Shogun, we could only regret that happy time when the ancient sages gathered with no other object than to talk of beauty in the heart of nature, in wonderful gardens in the midst of vegetation, luxuriant and restful, with the blue heavens as their sole canopy.

But our modern civilization has other necessities, which

find expression in a care, sometimes exaggerated, regarding subjection to the order of the hour: "Time is money"; it is necessary, then, that the time of the reunions should be limited, and that the place be carefully chosen, large enough to contain the public, which rarely would wish to assemble out of doors, lest the fine weather might change into a driving rainstorm.

It is of no use regretting things that cannot be changed; and it is wiser to listen to Yoritomo:

"I once knew a man who spent large sums in entertaining several Buddhist priests, who celebrated the cult by lighting an enormous quantity of lanterns, and by giving themselves up to various ruinous practices."

"I said to this man: 'It would be better to burn a single lamp before the statue of Buddha at his own home, and to invite all the priests who lead a useless existence in the temple to bear to the people the good word and to set them a good example.' "

"Put together all the money which every year you would give to this sterile cult of Buddhism, divide it into as many sums as you would distribute to each of your priests in ordering them to distribute it among their poor as they teach them of the blessings derived in the name of Buddha."

"Thus, glorified by example, the cult that you desire to honor would spread itself more, since kind and charitable words would inevitably be connected with it in the minds of the unfortunates whom it had helped."

"The ability of certain actors," Yoritomo continued, "may be an influence, excellent or detestable, following the quality of the examples which they offer to the people."

"On the stage, an actor who has the gift of filling his very soul with the personage he represents can, at his will, sow the seeds of joy or terror, of admiration or desire for the beautiful in the minds of the spectators."

"That is the reason why we cannot too strongly censure such plays which show a narrow or a vulgar mentality behind them."

"It is very wrong to impress the multitude with reproductions of criminal or reprehensible actions."

While it is true that there are certain lower functions of our human nature that are common to every one, but which we mutually conceal, both from sight and by name, there are certain moral defects, certain ugly actions, a manifestation of which it would be very wrong to present to the eyes of the public.

"Do not the acts of generosity, of magnanimous impulses, and of heroic sacrifices offer a field wide enough so that it is not necessary to reproduce plays of sentiments and actions that are likely to be harmful?"

"The influence of example is considerable, and it is a culpable thing not to circumscribe it to the representation of noble actions worthy of being imitated."

"It may be objected that in all plays in which a criminal is represented, male factors are always punished for their misdeeds, sometimes in a way so terrible that the example cannot fail to be of benefit as a warning to those that might be tempted to imitate them."

"That is an error common to those who occupy themselves with the study of psychology only in a superficial way."

"Among an audience capable of being influenced by these detestable examples, there are sure to be a few who will fancy themselves much cleverer than the criminals whose stories are being acted before them, and these will say to themselves: 'The crime was well-planned; and, if the perpetrators were taken, it is because they were clumsy.' "

"For many, these reflections are theoretical, and they have no desire to imitate them. But what matters that? The evil seed has been sewn in them and, under the influence of an unworthy sentiment, hatred, calculation, or cupidity, it may develop into a fixed desire for dishonest conquest, of which the pictured crime was the origin."

"For those who are already tainted, the influence of such representations as we are considering would be even more vicious; for them the stage would be a practical school of vice, combined with astuteness and safeguarded from punishment by a thousand means which the actions of the players may suggest."

"One may say the same thing of books, though they are more dangerous for the erudite than for persons whose knowledge is more limited."

Alas! the Shogun knew nothing about compulsory education, nor of the thousands of cheap books, which propagate the taste for trying one's luck in the convincing tone of showing one how to make a fortune.

But it would be wrong to include the spirit of a book, which deplores all progress, which we praise highly. We should, however, emphasize very clearly the fact, that too wide an education, is often a two-edged weapon.

In some cultures, particularly in areas where many people do not read themselves, teachers, preachers or others in the community may read books, articles or essays to groups. Such readings should be on subjects at once lofty and interesting; but the result on the auditors when they are alone may be indifferent or beneficial, according to the mental qualities of the readers.

The reader should, above all things, be inspired with the principal contents of the preceding chapters, particularly those on the influence of the eye and thought-transference. To maintain dominance over the audience, the reader should look up from the book from time to time to maintain eye contact with them.

"At the same time the ideas expressed should be backed by so powerful a thought from the reader that the thought-waves shall determine the mental current and act with the force of of electricity."

Let us not forget also that personal influence radiates more certainly when it manifests itself under the form of altruism, charity, and kindness.

"Is it not a frequent thing," said the old Japanese, "to see a crowd hesitate, divided between a feeling of recrimination and one of approbation, and then suddenly turn toward conciliation, because one among them, on whom the situation and the influence of others had its effect, has openly declared agreement with those who favor conciliation.?"

"One of the greatest obstacles to the doing of good actions," he added, "is the timidity based on the fear of responsibility, which haunts mediocre minds."

"It is toward these that those who would wield the power of domination should turn their attention. It is sufficient to impose on these timorous souls the resolution to perform the task that they themselves desire to see accomplished, and to set them the example of their achievements."

"Their vacillating will strengthen itself by the moral support which they will be certain to feel, and their anxiety about the opinion of others will be soothed by the example of those whom they recognize as their superiors, and whose superiority they are glad to acknowledge."

"Example is the excuse behind which hasten to hide those whose ill-regulated thoughts cannot cooperate in defensive discernment."

"It is these, then, whose minds are strengthened by renewed practices of wise reflection, used in the service of psychic qualities, creators of domination, who should watch carefully over their own acts, so that their example may be, for the persons over whom they have an influence, a source of improvement and constant elevation."

LESSON VI

By Psychic Influence

Psychic influence consists in awakening the forces, too often wasted by a habitual state of moral weakness, or perhaps lessened from a physiological cause.

It is the power that determines the processes that we wish to produce in other minds.

It is the art of substituting for the want of resolution in others, our own will, which they obey blindly, sometimes unconsciously, ever glad to feel themselves guided and directed by a moral power which they can not elicit in themselves.

"It is not necessary," says Yoritomo, "to have, as many pretend, recourse to magic in order to become past masters in the art of influencing others; what is needed above all is to keep ourselves constantly in a condition of will-power sufficient to impose our commands on minds capable only of obedience."

"Intensity of determination, when it reaches a certain point, possesses a dazzling influence which few ordinary mortals can resist, for it envelops them before they are aware of it and thus before they have dreamt of endeavoring to withdraw themselves from it."

"Moreover, those who retain the power of influencing rarely need to exert themselves, in order to exercise it effectually, for the need of protection from it, is non-existent in most persons."

"They are rare who are morally sufficient for themselves and who pass through life without feeling the need of resting their weakness on a supporting and directing force."

"Still less numerous are those who accept with courage the consequences of their acts and do not seek to place the responsibility for these acts on an outside influence, which, however, they are ready to repudiate if they are successful."

"But, should failure come, they will hasten to ascribe the causes to their advisers, proclaiming loudly that, if they had not been impelled to give ear to them, the disaster would not have come about."

"Timidity, while not influenced by the same motives, often leads those who suffer from it to such a dread of responsibility, that they arrive at the point of being unable to act, except under the shelter of an impelling power, the manifestation of which seems to them indispensable for excusing their activities."

"We might well pass over in silence, persons of bad faith, although they constitute an important group among those who seek the cooperation of others."

"But this sickly dependence on others is with them only adopted by design."

"Feeling themselves incapable of achieving anything by their own efforts, they are content to enjoy the fruit of the exertions of others, for they can always take credit to themselves for the best part, by throwing into the shade those who have a far better right to commendation than themselves."

"I once knew two brothers who were devoted to the study and explanation of the ancient inscriptions graven in temples by the hand of primitive faith."

"The younger of these brothers was verbose, very superficial, but a very brilliant and learned talker."

"The other, continually engrossed, kept himself almost entirely out of sight, uttered only words absolutely necessary, and, when questioned on his science, replied so simply that people pitied his brother for being burdened with such an obvious nonentity."

"The latter, however, won the, good graces of every one by never speaking of his elder brother except with respect and by displaying a certain uneasiness when his learning was discussed."

"In spite of everything, he was obliged to admit he alone was learned, and his brother too shallow to take any other role than that of copyist; but it was perceived that this declaration hurt his brotherly feelings, and the esteem conceived for him increased the more."

"Now the day came when the elder brother vanished into the spirit world; his death passed almost as unnoticed as his life, and no one dreamed of regretting him, when a serious mistake was discovered in a much-disputed text. Of course, the error fell on the memory of the copyist, that useless person whom the kindness of his brother had wished to class among the learned."

"The survivor appeared so affected by this that he gave up his work for some time, and his utterances grew dull and commonplace."

"Nevertheless, at the instance of his friends, he undertook the translation of some ancient Buddhist prayers of immense religious and archeological interest."

"Great was the general astonishment. The grossest errors were combined in this work with the most palpable ignorance; in short, it was impossible to doubt of this: not only had the dead brother merit alone, but he had also the gifts of influencing the younger, for, under the dazzling action of the elder one's thought, the other had been able to reflect himself to the extent of imposing on every one."

And Yoritomo adds:

"It is unquestionable that, by throwing off the effluvia of a sound mental perception, we are able to obtain results which material efforts would achieve with more difficulty."

"Nevertheless, it is sometimes indispensable to avail

ourselves of other powerful means in order to put in vibration, the forces which surround us and must cooperate in the creation of the result which we wish to attain."

"Every one knows that certain orders uttered during a sleep which we have brought on, continue after waking in the form of an obsession, at first confused, afterwards dim, but gaining in definiteness and at length tenacious, and, I should say, almost instinctive."

"The quickest and most scientific method of obtaining this sleep is the condition of torpor, produced by a look, in which we have learned to embody the fascination of our influence."

"I have already mentioned the power of this look, but we shall increase it in a remarkable degree, if we can succeed in approaching the persons whom we wish 'to influence by lightly touching their shoulders with our hands, turning the thumbs toward their necks and the finger-tips on their vertebral columns.' "

"If we are afraid to display too much the desire of influencing, and wish to avoid provoking a shrinking back, whether voluntary or not, it will be well to proceed by standing behind the persons whom we wish to put to sleep and, chatting the while, place both hands on their shoulders."

"But this procedure is more difficult to put in practice, for the application of the hands must last more than a minute in order to be efficacious."

"In any case, the experiment can only succeed if it is accompanied by putting forth a strong and fixed power of will."

"If you give to your thought the strength and fixity required, even though the persons whom you wish to put to sleep should not succumb to slumber, they would, nonetheless, become utterly subject to the mental processes which you have willed to arouse in them."

"But a single second of distraction would render all your exertions vain."

"In order to obviate this failure, it is then well to give to the thought, a tangible shape and not to abandon it to a meditative condition; it must take on the features of the object of the desire which you wish to inspire."

"For example, you desire to inculcate in some one the love of science, make a picture in your mind representing him or her, bending over manuscripts, or in the dim light of crypts, see that person engaged attentively in deciphering inscriptions, and seeking their meaning, that veritable key of the door from which the truths of history emerge."

"If you wish to imbue them with the warlike spirit, imagine them confronting enemies, whom they are crushing to earth."

"Similarly with every accomplishment the idea of which you wish to see born in their minds."

"At the same time, it is absolutely necessary to accentuate and to sustain the thought by words that rouse and stimulate it, by a definite enunciation of it."

"For example, you will say to the person whom you wish to render brave and resolute: 'Lift your head and accustom yourself to look danger in the face; flee not, it would pursue you and surely overtake you; but know how to measure yourself with it and confront it with a countenance unblanched with fear.' "

"It is with such words uttered in a firm voice, while using the influence of the eye, that of the thought and that of the will, combined with the power of the fluids, that you will succeed in subjugating the most rebellious natures and in making the most inattentive give ear."

"Leaders should never lose sight of this truth: the effort of the will produces vibratory waves, the circulation of which, must touch the brain of those whom they wish to subjugate."

"To allow this force the means of unbending a little, it is well, when you engage in conversation, to remain quiet while the others talk."

"While listening to them with attention, you will avoid looking at the speakers and, without affectation, turn your eyes from theirs, in order not to allow to be scattered, the fluid, which later you will send forth more efficaciously, if, instead of submitting involuntarily to the sway of the speech coming from your interlocutor, you reserve the accumulation of your psychic forces to support your discourse with all the power of occult insight."

"This must be strictly observed when it involves imposing a definite resolution, such as to deter one from a blamable action, or one contrary to that which you desire to see follow."

"Then, persuasion by influence takes the form of suggestion, and, after having had recourse to the practices which we have just described, you should say, fixing your eyes, not on but between the bridge of the nose: 'You will not do such or such a thing, because that is bad and would draw you into grievous ills;' or: 'You must do such a thing, there is the solution of the problem which you seek.' "

"If the desired result should not be obtained after a first trial, you should renew it."

"It is, however, preferable to press home the conviction gradually; it thereby gains solidity, and the vacillation, so common in feeble minds, is less to be feared in proportion as the suggestion has been slow in affirmation."

The Shogun deals also with the health of the body, which, he assures us, is always related to that of the mind, and recommends means for assisting the cure of certain sick persons.

Nevertheless, he advises the greatest care in the use of these agencies, however beneficent they may be.

"It is bad," he says, "roughly to compel imaginary invalids to recognize moral error, the prime cause of physical ailments."

"We should, on the contrary, refrain from denying the existence of their sufferings and, little by little, introduce into their minds the suggestion of something better, until the moment when the idea of recovery gains possession of them."

"But in order to acquire a definite value, this idea must be the culmination of a series of other thoughts, the upward gradation of which has led the patients to conceive, at first as a possibility, then as a well-grounded hope, afterward as a certainty, at last as a realization, the complete return of health definitely regained."

"Influence is synonymous with 'substitution of will'; in certain cases, the word 'creation' would be still more appropriate, for those whom we have succeeded in dominating to the extent of directing their thoughts, are nearly always persons of weak character in whom the faculty of volition has remained in a rudimentary state."

"As for the others, those in whose minds we substitute our own will for that which they tend to manifest, they are, generally, dull or frankly vicious souls, who combine with their natural defects a kind of moral weakness, which renders them accessible to outside influence."

"When two forces come together, it is oftener the evil one that gives way, for, to possess the genuine endowment of influence, certain qualities must come into play which rarely fall to the lot of mediocre minds."

"The latter, fatally enslaved to the satisfaction of their instincts, and their strength sapped with fleeting pleasures, lack that impassioned desire of the better, the creator of the cohesion of forces."

"The masters of conscious-will alone, can hope to arrive at this splendid goal of influencing others, for, their spirit being imbued with nothing but the love of truth, they will ignore those passing whims that ever imprint falsehood or deceit on the thought of those who love to stray along the devious bypaths of unworthy considerations."

"The latter must never hope to possess completely the power of dominance, for they ignore the unity of thought, in-as-much as their mouth utters one word while their mind conceives another; thus the image can not take shape in them except in an imperfect fashion, and we know how important a part that plays which we might call, in a way, the materialization of the idea in the art of influencing others."

"It is not given to all to possess in themselves the aggressive spirit necessary to command the influences which must emanate from our brain in order to result in forming the convictions of others; that is why it is sometimes well, instead of commanding the idea, to let it simply penetrate by itself, in order that we may arrive at its complete possession, which should not be confounded with the fact of being possessed by it."

"The difference is immense: those who possess completely the idea which they wish afterwards to send out by the means, which we have described in this chapter, in order to transmit the idea to others, are true leaders. Those who allows themselves to be overcome by the obsession of an idea which takes possession of their brains and prevents their reasoning, is the slave of that idea and of the acts which it will impel them to commit."

"But this cannot be, if quietly and by degrees, they allow themselves to be imbued with it, for the gradual conquest implies discussion, reasoning, and even resistance, things all indispensable to the formation of rational conviction."

"Now, without conviction, influence has little weight."

"It is personal conviction which allows us to find the words necessary to introduce it into the minds of our hearers; only personal conviction can produce adepts."

"All apostles have been persuaded of the truth of their belief, and, if some among them have been the leaders of the multitude, it is because they taught a doctrine in which they themselves sincerely believed and because their discourse spread around them, the radiance of fervor, which, far better than enthusiasm, can fill people's souls and influence them."

The gradual penetration of the idea is, therefore, to

be sought in the case of those, whom their natural qualities incline, rather to meditation and steady adherence than to aggressive zeal.

"We might compare these different characters to those two men who, having each obtained an equal supply of wood in the forest, returned home and lit the fire to warm themselves."

"One of them let the flames mount in beautiful spiral curves of prismatic color, and when they died down he threw in a fresh armful, delighted with the pleasure of the sight and with the bodily comfort of the warmth."

"But soon nothing remained with which to renew the fire; the flames died away; the ruddy fire took on a vesture of gray, then a fine ash, rapidly cooling, alone remained at the bottom of the fireplace."

"The man went out again to find a fresh supply; but in passing before the hut of his friend, he was astonished to see smoke arising from it, while near the threshold, the pile of wood still lay, but little diminished."

"He went in; an agreeable warmth took possession of him and he saw a modest fire gently smoldering under the ashes; all around people were standing stretching their hands for the genial sensation that pleasantly imbued them."

"So it is with gradual and continuous penetration; if it does not produce brilliant flashes, it bathes us with its beneficent suggestion, and persuaded at last that we bear within us the truth, it will be so much the easier for us to surround ourselves with all the means that the knowledge of influence places at our disposal for allowing this truth to filter gently into the minds of those who would seem to us worthy of understanding it and of spreading it in their turn."

LESSON VII

By Decision

We should not confuse the virtue of decision with that tendency which certain persons display to decide any question, whatsoever, without having studied it and too often without having understood it.

Like all qualities, decision is only acquired after repeated acts of reflection, determining the coordination of ideas and rendering those who devote themselves to it habitually ready to understand in a moment the advantages, at the same time as they perceive the disadvantages, of the acts which they propose to perform.

To attain this, we must take into account all the reasons indispensable for evolving decision,

"These reasons." said Yoritomo, "are always dependent on circumstances which constantly assume a new character; for it is rarely, indeed, that in our lives the necessity for the selfsame resolution makes itself felt on several occasions; even in the case in which the present emergency seems to reproduce exactly a former event, we shall find in the manner of viewing it, in the forecasting of the consequences, even in the gradual change of our feelings, a number of fine distinctions, which do not allow us to form the same opinion about it that we have in the past."

"In order to be able to discern and understand quickly to which side our decision ought to incline, in order above all to be able to sustain it, several qualities are necessary, at the head of which we should name:

- Reflection or concentration.
- Presence of mind.
- Will.
- Energy.
- Impartiality.
- Desire of justice.
- Forethought.

"Reflection, or rather concentration, is the faculty of self-recollection, of shutting ourselves away from every thought that is not the one that should engage our attention."

It is force that we bear within ourselves, but which we develop to its highest degree by cultivation and application.

"It is by the habit of reflection by which we succeed in reviewing, very rapidly, every side of a question and in weighing the pros and cons of the resolutions to be taken."

"This habit, when it is constant, becomes a kind of mental gymnastics and allows us to range together in the twinkling of an eye, the reasons which militate in favor of the conclusion, or those which should decide the abandonment of the project, which is proposed to us."

"When the balance carries it strongly to one side or the other, the decision is plainly indicated, but many cases arise in which the reasons in favor are quite as important and as numerous as those against, so that the undecided person stops to weigh them interminably."

"Those of us whom the regular practice of reflection has perfected, after having rapidly established this equilibrium, will withdraw our minds from these motives in order to summon others of a different order."

We will bring in questions of family, of convenience, of surroundings, we will weigh the consequences of acceptance against the inconvenience of refusal, and we will make up our minds in a clear fashion and one devoid of any regret.

"Now comes in the second factor - Will."

"It is sometimes very hard to reply by refusal to something which, in the midst of dangerous advantages, presents seductive aspects; it is painful also to undertake certain responsibilities and to bind oneself to onerous conditions."

"But those of us who are gifted with will accept this task with a light heart, for we know that we are worthy of discharging it."

"However, this faculty, that admirable origin of the forces that govern life, does not always suffice to fortify decisions, it needs, in order to sustain them, to call to its aid energy, which, by continuousness of effort, comes to prevent the faintness which might affect these decisions as time goes on."

"Is there need to insist on impartiality, the exercise of which is indispensable when considering one's innermost self?"

"The majority of the irresolute, love to deceive themselves by the delusions which their imagination creates, and thus become only too often the architects of their own misfortune."

"Or again the decision, sometimes too sudden, is dictated to them by one reason alone, which, with their tacit participation, takes on such gigantic proportions that it hides all the disadvantages, which they embellish, if they are forced to perceive them, with colors which they know to be fictitious."

"Sincerity is also necessary with ourselves as with others, and those who do not practice it regret sooner or later having disregarded it."

"It is from the same principle that the desire of justice proceeds, which should predominate in all our decisions, if we wish that they bring us no remorse."

"Blundering selfishness can only dictate resolutions which have no foundation in rectitude, for, sooner or later, regrets will arise for the acts that inevitably follow, and the concatenation of events will become the punishment of those who have neglected the laws of the love of their neighbor."

"The principal condition of decisions that leave no bitterness behind is the foreseeing of the events which these decisions may elicit."

"To foresee is to prevent, says an ancient maxim, and for want of foresight we often entrust ourselves to a quicksand where, in spite of every effort, we are miserably engulfed."

"We should not confound forethought with the art of divination, although, in the eyes of the vulgar, it sometimes takes on the appearance of it."

"Such persons, adept in rational reflection, are so advanced in this science that deduction takes the place of second sight, and they succeed in formulating predictions which might pass for prophecies, if they did not themselves take care to explain in what manner they have come to form their judgment."

"It is related that an ancient Mikado, pursued by ill fortune, assembled his soothsayers in order to obtain from them, the means, of averting the anger of the malignant spirits."

"After much discussion, they agreed that the only means of attaining this was to build a temple consecrated to the gods of Evil, in order to appease them by paying them honor; this temple was to be built on a spot indicated by the magicians."

"However, a preliminary sacrifice was demanded by the merciless gods; a child was to be slain and the temple to be erected on the place crimsoned by its blood."

"After lengthy cabalistic incantations, it was decided that this child should be the first whom chance led them to meet at daybreak in the neighboring forest."

"So the Mikado set out with the sorcerers and a numerous retinue."

"The sun had just risen over the horizon, when they saw through the branches a child walking and making a way for himself through the denseness of the thicket."

"To seize him and lead him to the Mikado was the work of a moment; the poor child was immediately subjected to an examination by the magicians who all agreed in declaring that his blood would be agreeable to the evil gods, and he was committed to the soldiers, who dragged him after them, cruelly divulging to him what would be the tragic end of his captivity."

"Neither prayers nor supplications availed to move any of these fanatics, and the party pursued its course as far as the foot of a hill that overlooked the sea."

"Arrived at this point, the Mikado and his retinue stopped, for it had been decided to choose the flat land covering this hill for the building of the temple."

"The soldiers began to convey thither an enormous stone which, after serving as an altar of human sacrifice was to be the foundation of the edifice."

"The child, seized with an anguish quite comprehensibly, followed with attention all these preparations; but in proportion as he formed an explanation of the work of the soldiers, his countenance cleared, an expression of hope lit up his face, and in a little while he asked permission to speak. Permission being granted him, he bowed three times before the Mikado and cried:

'O great prince, do not allow the work undertaken to proceed, for the gods of the forest are opposed to it.' "

"The Mikado who was superstitious, but not wicked, looked at him sadly : 'Child,' said, he, 'our soothsayers have decided it thus; it is the only means of appeasing the anger of the malignant spirits whose evil influences threaten the safety of the throne; it is painful to me to sacrifice so young a life, but the welfare of my empire depends on it; resign thyself and die bravely, in order to enter the realm reserved for the valorous.' "

"During this address, the child followed attentively the movements of the soldiers and all at once uttered a cry:

'Command them to stop, great prince, for a few steps

farther and the gods of the forest will destroy them.' "

"And turning toward the densely wooded forest:

'Gods of my childhood,' he entreated, 'ye who have ever protected me, give me a fresh proof of your beneficent protection by engulfing up my tormentors together with the altar on which they would sacrifice me.' "

"Hardly had he uttered these words than, as if by magic, the soldiers who were pushing forward the heavy stone disappeared - stone and all had been drawn into the bowels of the earth by an invisible power."

"The assemblage cried out at the miracle and hastened to cut the bonds of the captive, who was lost forthwith in the depths of the forest."

"It had sufficed him, for saving his life, to remember that, when pasturing his goats, he had been stopped by quicksand, which, had it not been for his nimbleness and lightness, would have made him their prey."

"To foresee that men rolling a heavy block of stone could not avoid being swallowed up, was thus easy for him, and this child accustomed to the devices of the simple, which at every moment must protect their lives, had contracted, in the solitudes of the forests, the habit of rapid decision in all that concerns this instinct of self-preservation, so highly developed in all primitive minds."

"Threatened with immolation by those who wished to appease barbarous gods, his astuteness had forced on him, the quick decision to strike awe into their minds by prophesying an event which foresight caused him to view, as inevitable."

"This is the case of many soothsayers, but it is above all that of sages, who only undertake an enterprise after they have foreseen its difficulties."

"Cells formed spontaneously as the result of chance are too often produced by circumstances."

"If it is difficult to foresee their nature, it is absolutely necessary to recognize them under the vague name of bad luck and to take into account their happening, in order not to be taken by surprise when they burst upon us."

In turning over a few more pages, we come upon a definition of decision, couched in brief and concise phraseology, such as the Nippon philosophy knows how to employ when it would sum up a thought in such a manner as to impress the mind.

"Decision," he said, "is not a spontaneous movement of the mind or of the intelligence, it is the coherent and rational choice of performing an act, to the exclusion of all others, which might bear a relation to the idea expressed."

And he adds:

"Between the moment when the reason for the decision appears and that in which it is a question of making the resolve, all the psychic states which separate these two periods find place."

"We have just enumerated them rapidly, but in order to grasp them in their integrity and to make them serve for the accomplishment of our projects maturely conceived and rapidly inaugurated, a kind of mental gymnastics is not unprofitable."

"For example, it is well to place ourselves in face of imaginary resolutions and to make up our minds while striving to do so as speedily and wisely as possible."

"It will be easy for us to measure the wisdom of our resolutions, if we take as our end the events which surround us and if we study the delicate cases which are within reach of our knowledge."

"It is well, on seeing arise among our friends circumstances of which we have no experience, to make use of them as a subject for our exercises and to say to ourselves: 'What decision should I make if I were faced with this problem?' "

"I do not say, mind you, that all the details of the facts would become known to you in such a way that it would be possible to reason from them with certainty."

"This method has the advantage of a check, for it allows

you to verify the success of the decisions which you have made in imaginary cases."

"You can thus instruct yourself in this art, so difficult and nevertheless so important, for the influence which those who are accustomed to wise and prompt decisions exert over others, is always considerable."

"Further, when some time you devote yourself to this study, you will come to make it naturally and without any effort."

"Clearness of mental vision will develop within you to such a point that, without giving it a thought, you will come to pass a sound judgment on everything and to discern quickly what is the proper solution to each."

"Soon the fame of your wisdom will spread abroad and the weak-willed ones will come to gather around you to ask your counsel."

"For they are numerous who dare not venture alone in the paths of will - the creator of responsibilities."

"Their craven souls fear the regrets arising from a resolution of which they would have to bear the consequences." He then related this allegorical adventure:

" 'A man,' he said, 'had to pass through a forest in order to reach a village where he hoped to meet Fortune.' "

"He set out very early in the morning and hastened to reach as quickly as possible the outskirts of the forest."

"But when he had walked for some hours, he stopped and looked around him in indecision; the road laid out was long and monotonous; by taking a by-path across the wood he had perhaps a chance to shorten it . . . and he lost his way under the great trees."

"He walked on for an hour and found himself in a glade. He tried to get his bearings, but, not knowing what to do, he took a road by chance. He went more slowly, for he began to feel fatigue and became quite dejected, when he perceived that the road had brought him back quite near to the point whence he had set out."

"He then took the opposite road, but he could not keep count of the windings that it made, so that after a long course he saw the glade again."

"That was for him, the moment of a great resolution, he gave up definitely the side roads and set out on the first road which he had followed and which led directly to the village."

"But the sun set behind the trees; night covered the forest with its veil, and the distracted man was obliged to interrupt his journey, now useless, for Fortune had failed to wait for him."

"Do not laugh at this man," cried the Shogun, "you are for the most part like him; you wander in the labyrinths of indecision instead of following the way pointed cut by the will; you lose your presence of mind at the first objection; you avoid being sincere with yourselves by avowing that you heedlessly lose your way in unknown roads, and when at length you pause before a definite course, opportunity has wearied of waiting for you."

"Despise these irresolute ones, ye who aspire to become those whose influence radiates over the souls of others."

"Be counselors with well-weighed and prompt decisions; do not stray in the by-paths of which you do not know the windings, and learn to become safe and enlightened guides for yourselves before pointing out the way to those of whom your influence has made attentive and devoted disciples."

It seems that to add any comment to these teachings would be to risk weakening them, for these appeals burning with energy, as well as the luminous illustrations that accompany them, can serve as a rule of conduct for the people of this day as well as for the far-distant disciples of Yoritomo.

LESSON VIII

By Rational Ambition

"Ambition is accessible only to the brave; they alone can discover the treasure hidden within it, by breaking up the sham gems of illusion and intrigue."

These words of Yoritomo should be known to all those who set out for the conquest of life.

They should be inscribed in letters of gold on the frontals of schools where the young make the initial start that, in most cases, decides their future.

"Ambition," again says the old philosopher, "should, equally with goodness or any other virtue, form the object of rational teaching."

"But for that it would be necessary to disengage ourselves from prejudices which brand it as a fault which we ought to dissemble."

"He or she is an ambitious one," say the vulgar, when they wish to discredit the achievements of a person whose aspirations raise that person above the commonplace things of life.

"They do not dream that, in order to form a genuine and productive ambitious person, it is necessary to possess a great number of qualities which people who pride themselves on their modesty, will always ignore."

"What is understood generally by modesty?"

"Is it the shrewd reserve of ambitious people who fear

to display their appetites in order not to be liable to restrain them before having found the means of satisfying them?"

"Is it not too often the sham virtue which, under the borrowed lineaments of humility, hides the terrible defect of weakness?"

"Would it not rather be the tinsel in which idleness likes to dress itself up in order to abandon itself with ease to its favorite vice?"

"Modesty can serve as a standard for all the vices which we have just mentioned; it is the enemy of courageous undertakings, of acts that require a display of energy that ambition or boldness alone can decide on."

"It is besides, nearly always, the sign of a want of confidence in oneself."

"It is again the safeguard of the self-respect of the incapable."

"Many weak mortals, irresolute, idle, or incompetent, instead of seeking to acquire the qualities which they lack, prefer to declare loudly: 'Oh, as for me, I shall never succeed in attaining this end, for the good reason that I shall not undertake it. I am a modest person, I am. I have a hatred of fame and renown surrounding my name; I desire only obscurity, and I pity keenly all those who are tormented by a desire to shine!"

"They say all this without thinking that the first condition of the being of modesty consists in ignorance of its existence."

Those who pride themselves on modesty will never be truly modest, for the moment they set out to establish their virtue, they act like braggarts.

"If they are really convinced of their unimportance, if their diffidence is sincere, we should pity them very keenly, for they will suffer in feeling so insignificant, and this feeling will lead , little by little, to hypochondria, unless they incline to the side of jealousy."

"Such is almost without exception, the punishment of

the weak; they have not themselves courage to undertake great things and they do not forgive those who achieve them."

"There is, however, a kind of modesty before which we ought to bow; it is that of the learned person who, finding happiness in the quest of knowledge and truth, makes no attempt to gain glory, and waits in the midst of his or her apparatus and parchments for it to develop, while preparing to welcome it with no more emotion than an ordinary visitant."

"This sentiment would be worthy of admiration, if it were not so often mingled with an inveterate selfishness, behind which is hidden an indifference toward others, carried to the point of excluding anxiety to cause others to share in the benefit of one's discoveries."

"This kind of modest person who ignores thus, his or her duty toward others, is less useful to humanity than an ambitious person, who, eager to become famous, will make known the result of what is accomplished to the sound of the trumpet."

"For in order to be fruitful, everything in our life must bear relation to others."

"It is by developing ambition in their breasts that the leaders of the multitude have succeeded first in gaining a hearing and then in carrying conviction."

"What generous impulse can we expect from those who have only one desire; to shut themselves up in the selfish quiet of a life, the works of which they jealously keep to themselves?"

These facts, already true enough in the days of the Shogun, assume a fresh significance in our time, when they might become the textbook of those whom we designate by the name of those who have arrived and who are in the majority of cases nothing if not ambitious ones - I was almost going to say the rightfully ambitious.

And why? Ambition, when it excludes unworthy means and spurns intrigue, is it not one of the noblest passions that could be conceived?

National ambition furnishes our projects with wings that allow them to mount above commonplace ideas; it is thanks to ambition that we experience emulation that carries us along the better way.

Without ambition should we have knowledge of those marvelous discoveries that make our age that of progress par excellence? And it might be said that Yoritomo set forth the splendid incentives given to the ambitious of our time by benefactors keen beyond measure on improvement, when he says:

"It is a crime to destroy in the breasts of children, under the pretense of modesty, that self-confidence which should shine like a star in the hearts of all."

"It would be more useful, on the contrary, to found rewards for distribution to those who, with a noble end in view, devote themselves to undertakings sometimes called rash."

"Such are the veritable handmaids of destiny, since, by their desire for the better, they sometimes succeed in discovering an improvement which ameliorates the lot in life of others..."

"Besides, it is well that every effort should be rewarded by an increase in the possessions of those who have made the attempt and who, by their special qualifications, have promoted a success, the good results of which are never limited to themselves."

"Justice demands that inventors should derive profit from their inventions, this will allow them to devote more of their time to the pursuit of another discovery."

It will perhaps be objected that there are some ambitious people who produce nothing. Those whose success profits only themselves cannot spread around them, the joy, which arises from generous benefactions.

The world is certainly peopled with a large number of selfish persons and it will, assuredly be, difficult to prevent this state of things, but it would be a serious mistake to believe that these people are, altogether, useless.

Ambition is never without the great desire of attaining everything which gratifies it, and what better means is there of proclaiming its success than to command a large retinue, to give banquets, and to build palaces, or plant spacious gardens?

Even granting that ambitious people who have attained satisfaction are hard-hearted and neglect works of charity, do not the workers who labor in providing the trappings of their vanity, profit largely by an ambition, which procures for them the means of subsistence?

By the law of human evolution, the money obtained by the ambitious will come of necessity to ameliorate the condition of the humble, in the same way as their works and their discoveries will always succeed in increasing the fund of public knowledge, for only modest people are able to keep to themselves, the result of their labors.

Those who would master fame or fortune, on the other hand, hasten to make public the most trifling success; true, they sometimes exaggerate it, but the fault is not theirs alone; it may be imputed to the habit of disparaging those, on whom, Fortune seems to smile.

"I heard one day," said the Shogun, "a man whom I knew to be of a serious turn of mind relate that he had spent three years in completing a work."

"Now I had followed his studies with interest, and I knew that this task had required of him in all a hundred and fifty days."

"I was, therefore, astonished, and questioned him on the reason of a falsehood which puzzled me, the more that I knew his habitual truthfulness."

" 'Child,' replied he, 'do you not understand that if I were to admit spending so little time in perfecting my work, people would not fail to find it incomplete or too lightly thought out? It is not sufficient to be capable, we must not shock any one in proving overmuch, this capability. For this assertion of a quality that they do not possess, causes suffering in the envious, who do not fail to revenge themselves for it, by belittling it to others. It is their method of succeeding in placing themselves in the same class; unable to rise to the level of people of merit, they try to bring the latter down to their level.' "

Ambitious people escape these cheap devices; they are from the first, too full of their projects, to give time to insignificant jealousies.

In short, they rarely resent the sentiment of envy, for they are always convinced that they will succeed in surpassing the success of those who are competing for the same goal.

Moreover, ambition is a sure and swift means of influence.

This is, in the first place, because people have always a tendency to follow those who draw them in the direction of light and progress. They are chosen to attain honors and fortune, and are almost always drawn from the following of the ambitious.

It forms no part of the program of the successful ones to drag after them, the incapable or weak; this is why their influence over their pupils extends the more in proportion as the latter imitate and follow them.

For, ambitious people are not displeased to see disciples raise themselves and perhaps some day, step into their vacant place. And here is one of the primary reasons for the influence which rational ambition can exert on the minds of people.

The lure of gain or distinction binds people to the train of those who are in a position to give such encouragement to them.

It is in their power to be able to employ this influence profitably for disseminating good and the love of the better around them; it is in their power to instill into the hearts of their devotees, aspirations toward a noble end; it is in their power always to put them on their guard against intrigues which would have the effect of diminishing the beauty of their ambition.

There is between ambitious people and intriguers, all the difference, that separates beauty from ugliness.

The first proceed directly toward a definite goal that they have long and maturely decided to choose; they disdain paltry methods; they seek only to attain the end that they have set up.

They move ahead with full confidence, sustained by a faith that is never lost from view, not withstanding the clouds that hide it from time to time.

They ignore the vulgar herd of the envious who swarm around them, unless, overmuch beset or tormented by their incessant attacks, they crush them under foot, as we do with an importunate insect, which we try at first to drive away and which we destroy, without ill feeling, simply to rid ourselves of its repeated and irritating stings.

Intriguers, on the other hand, rarely raise themselves above the horde of mean desires and paltry jealousies.

Unlike their ambitious counterparts, they act with no other end in view than procuring for themselves, money or pleasure.

No lofty thoughts ever enter their heads, longer than the time necessary to turn it to account, while considering only its mercenary aspect, and this accomplished, they pass to a class of ideas, the burden of which is ever the same.

The desire of distinction never haunts the dreams of intriguers; they reduce everything to the narrowness of their aspirations and entertain no project, that does not lend itself to their base sentiments.

Is that to say that we should despise money and seek after poverty?

"Not so," said Yoritomo, "for the poor person exercises little influence over the multitude."

"Again, most achievements demand considerable application and loss of time, and we could not lavish it in this way if we were obliged to take thought for the earning of our daily bread."

"It is, therefore, well to find resources that will allow the pursuit of an end without being compelled to give it up in order to provide for the necessities of daily life. This will also save us from compromises of conscience which the greatest leaders must sometimes endure, when they do not possess that advantage, indispensable to those who do not wish to diverge from their course, assurance as to the primary needs of life."

"This should be the first aim of those who wish to win honor, fortune, or distinction."

"Before rushing forth on toilsome paths on the chance of meeting such, we should be sure of the possibility of pursuing them and not risk missing them because the necessity of providing for our daily wants compels us to pause just when we had hoped to attain them."

We cannot but admire once again, the wisdom of Yoritomo, who once more is found in agreement with the greatest thinkers.

The ancient Greek poet, Theognis said: "The man who is broken down by poverty can neither speak nor act; his tongue is tied and his feet are chained."

It is only too true; downright poverty is a disadvantage, for it often compels those who suffer to pay court to the fortunate ones of this world.

In any case, it is a hindrance to all undertakings that require sustained effort and peace of mind, which can only be obtained by those certain of the morrow.

But, you will say, everybody cannot be rich, and many, becoming so, have known poverty; is it not then an insuperable obstacle?

Again the Shogun will reply to us:

"Poverty," said he, "is a hindrance only if it consists in absolute want, and in this case, it is usually the result of idleness or of mismanagement of our affairs."

"We should not reckon as poor people who earn a scanty livelihood, but whose peace of mind cannot be changed by the suffering resulting from the lack of necessaries."

"Such people can, when they have fulfilled the duties of their station in life, devote themselves to the aspirations of a lawful ambition."

"But the really poor are those who lack assured means, however small."

"Rarely do they enjoy independence, for in order to live, they must accept many humiliations or spend a considerable portion of time in quests, which have as their object, the insurance of sustaining a livelihood."

"If they are sincere in these efforts, they will not long remain poor, for they will soon find employment, no matter what, and if endowed with ambition, they will quickly succeed in distinguishing themselves in it."

From that time, poverty will be nothing but a specter of the past, for they will work to better their positions and will soon become successful.

Prosperity begins in the mind and is impossible while the mental attitude is hostile to it. It is fatal to work for one thing and to expect something else, because everything must be created mentally first and is bound to follow its mental pattern.

You can never become prosperous if you expect to remain poor. We tend to get what we expect, and to expect nothing is to get nothing. When every step you take is on the road to failure, how can you hope to arrive at the success goal?

It is facing the wrong way toward the black, depressing, hopeless outlook, even though we may be working in the opposite direction that kills the results of our effort.

Thoughts are magnets that attract things like themselves. If your mind dwells upon poverty and disease, it will bring you poverty and disease. There is no possibility of your producing just the opposite of what you are holding in your mind, because your mental attitude is the pattern, which is built into your life. Your accomplishments are achieved mentally first.

The terror of failure and the fear of coming to want and of possible humiliation, keep multitudes of people from obtaining the very things they desire, by sapping their vitality and incapacitating them, through worry and anxiety, for effective, creative work necessary to give them success.

The habit of looking at everything constructively, from the bright, hopeful side, the side of faith and assurance, instead of from the side of doubt and uncertainty; and the habit of believing the best is going to happen, that the right must triumph; the faith that truth is bound finally, to conquer error, that harmony and health are the reality and discord and disease, the temporary absence of it - this is the attitude of the optimist, which will ultimately reform the world.

I have never known anyone who believed in him or herself and constantly affirmed this ability to do what was undertaken, who always focussed on the goal and struggled determinedly towards it, who did not make a success of life. Aspiration becomes inspiration and then realization."

"Poverty is only allowable if it is voluntary, that is to say, if it is the result of a decision which prefers that condition to another more brilliant but less independent."

"Nevertheless, riches are the key of many marvels and they are above all the key of many influences."

"Not only are those of great possessions in a better position to make those, whom they patronize, listen to their words, but the prestige of their success surrounds them with a halo of influence, which, if they are wise, will be used to better the lot of other people."

"We do not receive kindnesses from an empty hand; we have nothing to expect from a person tormented by care for the morrow."

"What words can fall from a mouth sealed by hunger?"

It is true that fortune, considered simply from the point of view of riches, is not an exalted ideal, but we must nevertheless welcome it as the consecration of success and as a power of which, the sage knows how to dispose for the good of all people.

It is a means of exciting interest and of influencing the multitude, for the people will always be disposed to listen to the advice of those who have had the ability to acquire great possessions.

It is then in the power of those, who have been able to acquire, this power of money, to make use of it for establishing a beneficent influence over the minds of those who are disposed to trust in them.

After their other successes, this last will not be a matter of indifference to those, who, while monopolizing the empire of the purse, will be proud to endeavor after the authority of the empire of the mind.

Thanks to the prestige which their riches confer on them, they will be able to spread the rays of influence, as far as, the boundaries of the attraction of thought, and as it displays itself above all in action they will gather around them, a band of brave and intelligent people, ready to imitate them in spreading abroad the ideas which they inculcated in them and to speak as they have taught them.

"Do not wait for the desired object to come to you, but rise up and set out to look for it; when you have found it you will undertake its conquest, and when it becomes your possession, you will gather together your friends to make them share in your good fortune and to tell them by what means it has befallen you."

In acting thus, you will follow the teaching of Yoritomo who said: "Ambition is a gate opening on magnificent gardens, but the fortunate ones who have entered it should not pause there; they will pass beyond the entrance in order to survey the road and to make a sign to passers-by, pointing out to them the way."

And this profound psychologist adds:

"A discovery brings no real joy to its finder until he or she can announce it, and we should rejoice at this almost universal law, for it is the cause of an improvement evolved by ambition, the happy influence of which awakens the instinct of conquest dormant in the breast of every righteous person."

LESSON IX

By Perseverance

Like persuasion, like good example, perseverance is among, if not the most brilliant, at least the most active agents of influence.

It is a faculty borne within them by people conscious of their power, those who, by virtue of faith in their own merit, advance to achievement with that confidence which gives birth to all notable successes and all productive achievements.

Perseverance is the triumph of will-power over the weakness of the will; it is the result of a profound study of the determining causes, the combination of which is bound to end in success; it is, in short, the slow but sure ascent toward a goal, that assumes a more definite shape, the nearer we approach it.

Few persons are born with a silver spoon in their mouths, but everybody can aim at conquering fortune by a series of continual and rational efforts.

The athlete who would spring up thirty feet at a single leap would spend a lifetime in ridiculous attempts, but if that athlete wishes steadily to mount the steps that lead to that height, it will be attained, sooner or later, according to the dexterity, the agility, and the perseverance which that person displays.

The steps, it is true, are often made of shaky stone; they have gaps between them that make one dizzy, where they are so uncertain that it is difficult to keep a foothold on them.

This is the point where those who possess the virtue of perseverance make themselves known; by their unshakable will they can ward off every danger; they balance themselves on the shaky stones almost on tiptoe and advance onto the next step; they feel fascinated by the giddy depths beneath them, quickly they raise their heads, they proceed gazing on their star, and they guard themselves against possible slips by making sure of one foot before lifting the other from the ground.

Even those with small ability will often succeed if they have the dogged persistence, where a genius without it would fail. Persistence wedded to character is the key to success in life. Money, influence, position are nothing as compared with brains, principle, energy and perseverance.

No one can pursue a worthy object steadily and persistently, with all the powers of one's mind, and yet be a failure. Focus the rays of the sun in winter, and you can kindle a fire with ease.

"For perseverance is the mother of many gifts; from her is born circumspection which clasps hands with application and patience."

"It is incredible to what degree the person who is gifted with patience is proof against the pitfalls of fate; hope and cheerfulness are two unanswerable arguments under most circumstances; application comes to hold up their hands, and few undertakings can resist their combined influence."

"It is related that the great scholar Yuan-Shi, plagued by the sour temper of his wife, who was jealous of his knowledge, could find no way of working at home, for this shrew went so far as to throw his manuscripts about and burn the sheets of paper on which he set down his thoughts."

"He, therefore, resolved, when he was at home, to divide his time between gardening and contemplation."

"But from the time that he got into the sedan car which conveyed him daily from his country house to the town where he was employed, he made up for the time lost by his enforced inactivity; and produced, after some months, a work of great value, which was, universally, commended and admired."

"News of this reached his wife, who asked him astoundedly, how he found the time to write, considering that outside his professorship, he was not engaged in any intellectual occupation."

"Yuau-Shi was a simple soul; he related to her how he had managed to reconcile his work with her unreasonableness."

"She was so affected by this proof of his desire not to annoy her, and so impressed by the calm and indomitable will of her husband, that from that day she ceased to forbid him to engage in work which brought him distinction, which shed its rays upon her in the form of caresses that saved her wifely self-respect."

This power persist is characteristic of all people who have accomplished anything great; they may lack in some other particular virtue, have many weaknesses or eccentricities, but the quality of persistence is never absent from successful people. No matter what opposition is faced or what discouragement arises, drudgery cannot disgust them; misfortune, sorrow, and reverses cannot harm them. It is not so much brilliancy of intellect, or fertility of resource, as persistency of effort, constancy of purpose, that make great people.

Those who succeed in life are the men and women who keep everlastingly at it, who do not believe themselves geniuses, but who know that if they ever accomplish anything, they must do it by determined and persistent industry.

John J. Audubon, the noted American ornithologist tells this story about himself: "An accident which happened to two hundred of my original drawings nearly put a stop to my researches on ornithology. I left the village in which I was living to go to Philadelphia on business. I looked to my drawings before departure, placed them carefully in a wooden box and gave them in charge of a relative with instructions to see that no injury would happen to them. My absence was for several months."

"When I returned, I inquired about my box and what I was pleased to call, my treasure. The box was produced and opened. To my dismay, a pair of rats had taken possession of the whole and reared a young family among the gnawed bits of paper, which had previously represented drawings of nearly a thousand birds. The burning heat that instantly rushed through my brain was too great to be endured without affecting my entire nervous system. I slept for several nights and the days passed like days of oblivion - until the animal powers being recalled into action through the strength of my constitution, I took up my gun, my notebook and my pencils and went forth into the woods, as if nothing had happened. I felt pleased that I might now make better drawings than before. Over the next three years, I filled my portfolio again."

This was similar to an experience of Sir Isaac Newton, whose accidental destruction of his papers when his little dog upset a lighted taper upon his desk, by which the elaborate calculations of many years were in a moment destroyed. Although, the loss seriously impaired his health and his mind, he persisted in reconstructing the work.

All are familiar with the misfortune of Carlyle while writing his "History of the French Revolution." After the first volume was ready for the press, he loaned the manuscript to a neighbor, who left it lying on the floor, and the servant girl took it to kindle the fire. It was a bitter disappointment, but Carlyle was not one to give up. After many months of poring over hundreds of volumes of authorities and scores of manuscripts, he reproduced that which had burned.

Do we reckon, what might be the production of one hour a day, won from frivolous pursuits to which we give so many precious minutes, which are so many drops of our life fallen into the gulf of eternity?

"The person," said the Shogun, "who should cut down a branch every day would end by clearing a way through the densest forest."

And he adds judiciously:

"But that person should not think of going back, for the branches grow again and the way would be closed."

That is to say that perseverance must never slacken; return is not allowed to those who should widen the road for their disciples to follow, and we cannot repeat too often.

The giants of the race have been people of concentration, who have struck sledgehammer blows in one place until they have accomplished their purpose. The successful people of to-day are those with one overmastering idea, one unwavering aim, one of single and intense purpose.

Thousands of people have been failures in life because they did not go quite far enough. They fail to walk that extra mile. They did not quite learn a trade to the point of efficiency; in other words, they stopped just this side of success.

It is by the power of personal effort and of application, that the most brilliant and solid reputations are slowly formed.

"Experience," says G. A. Mann, "tells us that we must have, in order to succeed, method in everything that we do and also perseverance; if we do not possess these two qualities we should develop them, by thinking constantly of them and by contemplating the idea which represents them."

"Persevere then! To what end, do you say? Simply because by persevering you form your will and besides have the chance of attaining your end."

"Persevere like a brute? Not at all. It is necessary that, in continuing what you have begun, your will, your intelligence, your sensibilities be ever on the alert."

"It is this unceasing activity in yourself, that is the reward of your effort."

"The road on which you walk may, perhaps, not lead you where you wished to go. But probably it will lead you to a better place. And for your walk, you will become a good walker, which will be certainly due to the impulse that you needed to be able to attain the goal, that is to say, success."

"Will without perseverance and without method could not exist."

Perseverance admits of a combination of active qualities and of virtues that might be called passive, for they demand no apparent effort.

Nevertheless, they are rarer than one might think, for they are not often the endowment of weak minds.

The latter can only, with difficulty, concentrate themselves on a task that requires a little application; they are the slaves of the instability of their impressions; beginnings, however arduous, always find them full of enthusiasm, but this fervor soon grows cold, and if success does not present itself immediately, they will hasten to give up their project and devote themselves to another, which will soon have a like ending.

Unremitting action can also be reckoned in the number of these virtues, passive indeed but indispensable, of which we have just spoken.

The practice of bending the will to listen to some purpose is sometimes a talent of a high order, for it is one of the best means of winning the sympathies of those who are speaking with us.

"I hate," said Yoritomo, "the sort of people who let their thoughts wander blindly instead of seeking to glean profit from what they hear."

"Nothing is more disconcerting than to feel the attention of those to whom you are speaking, drifting away and wandering after their thoughts, while you would like to convince them by your words."

"This lack of attention is always the mark of a vacillating will which can not bring itself to follow an idea by concentrating its mental powers on an examination of the various aspects which it presents."

"When dealing with inferiors, this frivolous inattention may pass as a sign of contempt; besides, it is always in opposition to the influence which we might exercise over them."

"What should we think of a squire whom a poor peasant comes to consult and who, instead of listening kindly, should pay little attention, as I have often seen, and give orders to servants and arrange the hangings of the house and let musicians go on playing?"

The unfortunate peasant would go out of the squires house with a bad impression, and if ever help or advice was needed in the future, would take care not to go a second time to the squire who treated the request with studied disdain.

"Influence over others is acquired especially by perseverance of the will and concentration of thought, the undulations of which, projected around us, come to reach the minds which we wish to impress."

And, entering once more into the domain of psychology, the Shogun speaks to us of this fascinating mystery of the contagion of thought, which according to him is a primary cause of influence and cannot fail by persevering determination to produce it:

"There is no doubt," he said, "that thought is a contagious factor of influence, good or bad."

"Who has not had occasion to remark this in the case of fear?"

"In an assemblage composed of the bravest people that it is possible to meet, taken individually, one person stricken with fear, if by expressing this fear in a forcible manner, will succeed in imparting to each of the rest, in different degrees it may be, the disquietude and uneasiness which he or she experiences."

"There are few doughty warriors who at the recital of something concerning the mysteries of the world beyond, have not felt a slight shiver which the sight of wholesale carnage, together with the consciousness of the gravest perils, could not have caused them to experience."

"This phenomenon, caused by the irradiation of thought, is an undeniable proof of the influence which it can exercise, for not only is it possible to penetrate the minds touched by the undulations of our own thought, but the thought of others, elicited by ourselves, comes back to us on the same undulations that are spread out from our brain."

"This is why we often see people who wished to shed fear around them feel that same fear by receiving the waves of thought that they have produced in their audience."

"It is the same with laughter."

"Very few are they who can resist the infection of a burst of laughter; even with those least inclined to merriment, laughter is infectious in a high degree; for at first, involuntary, in a way mechanical, it ends by becoming natural, so that, at the moment it breaks out, the simplest expressions, the most sedate words assume in the imagination, so comical an aspect, that merriment increases to the point of not being able to utter them without provoking a fresh outburst."

"But what happens if the next day we wish to relate this incident?"

"No longer submitted to the attractive influence of the thought of others, no longer receiving from them the undulations, the vibrations of which had reached us on the previous day, our state of mind is completely different, we perceive the inanity (sometimes we should say the foolishness) of what had amused us so highly on the preceding day, and no longer laughing over it ourselves, it is impossible for us to entertain others with it."

"On the other hand, if the story-teller - either of set purpose or spontaneously - begins by laughing at the remembrance of what is about to be related, it is seldom that this merriment, if it appears genuine, does not spread to others, who will laugh at first by infection, afterward of necessity, because merriment is the pervading thought."

"What we have just said on the subject of fear or of

laughter applies to everything else."

"With perseverance, you succeed in causing effectively to penetrate the minds of your hearers, the thoughts, the emission of which will attract similar thoughts, and their undulations returning to affect you will increase your conviction, giving you, thus, the more power to spread it around you."

It is from this standpoint that the Shogun sets out to oppose the emission of evil thoughts.

"It is" said he, "a weapon which always recoils on those who would make use of it."

The evil thought traverses the same cycle as the other and returns to us strengthened with hatred for others.

"What can we expect from those in whose minds we cause to germinate wickedness and the desire of evil?"

"As soon as they believe themselves capable, it is against us first of all that they will seek to exert themselves, and they will do it involuntarily by bringing back to us our thought, magnified and disfigured, so that we shall endure it without recognizing it."

"You see why perseverance should only be applied to the gaining of good, and as soon as we think we have come into association with it, it will be our duty to inculcate its principles into those who, living around us, are subjected to our influence."

"But we must not limit our efforts to this; we must aim farther and higher; it will not suffice to initiate them into good things, we must also give them the taste to cultivate them, and to that end, arouse in, them the desire of perseverance, which makes possible the most difficult undertakings and gives us a power that we cannot limit."

"Like some steel implement, the drop of water perforates the rock, wears away the hardest stone, and, without slacking, pursues this work which the implement would have begun more successfully perhaps, but the breaking or wearing out of the tool would have interrupted, perforce, the work which the eternal drop of water accomplishes by the tenacity and perseverance of its action."

"Do not then, seek to force slow-moving minds, but surround them, penetrate them by your perseverance, and its influence, sometimes obscure but always certain, will spread itself abroad in beneficent undulations, the continuance of which will create power."

Oliver Wendell Holmes expressed this well:

"Never give up, there are chances and changes,
Helping the hopeful, a hundred to one;
And, through the chaos, High Wisdom arranges
Ever success, if you'll only hold on
Never give up; for the wisest is boldest,
Knowing that Providence mingles the cup,
And of all maxims, the best, as the oldest,
Is the stern watchword of 'Never give up!' "

LESSON X

By The Prestige Gained from Concentration

Concentration is one of the most marvelous forces that can be conceived.

Without concentration, no success is possible; if it is present, we must consider it as the work of chance, not reckon too much on its duration, and remember the popular proverb that says:

"The person who comes to the sound of the flute goes back to the sound of the drum."

In other words, what a chance circumstance has brought, may depart on the wings of an unforeseen happening.

Far different is the success that we acquire by reason that, having sought it and willed it with all our powers, we have strained every effort to evoke it and no longer hug it to ourselves, for fear that it should leave us.

Fidelity to an idea is always the initial step to all successes.

For if an idea has no time to become at home with us, if what is rightly called the crystallization of thought does not form the foundation of every decision, we shall find it impossible to give it definite shape, and it will fade away like impalpable smoke.

If, on the other hand, we know how to exercise

concentration, this idea will soon become a focus of organization around which the association of ideas will come to marshal the reasons that determine the action that we have in mind.

"Thoughts are things," said the nineteenth century philosopher, Prentice Mulford; It is easy to imagine how true the saying is, seeing that in thinking deeply on a subject, we succeed in picturing it to ourselves in an almost tangible fashion.

The concentrated mind owns itself. It is the divine thinker of its own thoughts, and it declares just what kind of food the mind shall feed upon; it sets a guard upon its field of consciousness and will not allow a thought that is less than constructive to enter in. It picks up the thoughts which will reveal to it a perfect plan of life, then projects a perfect image of that plan and, standing firmly by its own creations, it fashions them again and again with increasing skill, until the whole structure of the self is brought into harmony.

"There is no doubt," said Yoritomo, "that concentration develops all our senses and brings them to a degree of remarkable acuteness."

"It stands to us in the stead of knowledge, for by its means we acquire the facility, that is to say the gift, of realizing readily and easily the things of which we have formed a conception."

"There is no work, even manual, that concentration does not lighten for us."

"If a you have to lift a heavy mass, do you think that you will do it as well if you are occupied with some other thought; as if you said, simply and solely:

'I wish to lift this mass' "

"Then your nerves are at tension, all your faculties bend themselves to the act with a force necessary to perform it; your brain strives after the means to assist the physical effort, for the muscles are the slaves of the will. By concentrating yourself on manual labor, you are certain to perform it with a minimum of fatigue, for you will be able to husband your strength and will save yourself from dissipating them in useless exertions. You will concentrate all your faculties of attention, of calculation, of ingenuity, and of muscular power in order to succeed."

"This is how so many jugglers achieve perfection in their art; by concentration, they have reached such a point of self absorption, that for them, nothing exists outside their own particular performance."

"But if one day in a fit of passion, they allow their thoughts to wander toward the object of their anger or of their love, they find that they are no longer themselves; their actions become less sure, they make bungle and end by being unable to regain their nerve, except with a violent effort that drives away the fancy and allows them to recall their thoughts to the one point, where they should keep them."

"To think of the act which we are performing, to think of it alone, to concentrate everything, and forget everything outside of it, there is the secret of so many successes, the explanation of so many good fortunes, that also of the immense influence which certain people exert over others."

"We must," said the Shogun, "be able to concentrate ourselves on one act at a time and to force our attention to the fullest degree to the manner in which, we can attract others to imitate us."

"We are the shapers of our destiny, and we should aspire to become shapers of the destiny of others."

"To gain this end, nothing should appear insignificant to us, and if we think sensibly, we shall see that every one of our acts, however commonplace it may seem to us, is, if it is performed with the desire of good, a step toward a realization, sometimes imposing, the fate of which, however, depends on a series of similar acts, equally paltry taken separately, but essential; for the inadequacy of one of them, might mar the perfection of the whole, if not jeopardize success altogether."

And in his flowery language, the Shogun adds:

"What is one link more or less in a chain several meters long? So trifling a thing that its absence would not be noticed. Nevertheless, if this link is badly riveted, this insignificant detail will suffice to break the chain."

"Every work is made up of a chain of acts more or less infinitesimal; the perfection of each of them contributes to that of the whole and it sometimes suffices for a slight slackness in the performance of one of these acts to jeopardize the success of an undertaking."

In fact, which of us has not had to regret a negligence, which has come to hinder the success of a project?

In our age of electricity and of strenuous life, these remarks are still more true than they would be at any other time.

Does it not happen every day that a missed train causes us the loss of the benefit of some business, which because of the delay escapes us?

Now, if we wish to be perfectly sincere with ourselves, we shall admit that, on most occasions, this delay is due only to our own carelessness; we were too late for meals, or we wasted time in talk which it would have been quite easy for us to curtail.

All the trouble arose from want of concentration, which allowed us to lose sight of the one thing that should have been for us of the first importance.

If we will reflect well on it, we shall see that most of our troubles can be set down to carelessness.

Take, if you wish, the case that we have just mentioned: A missed train prevents the settlement of an important business.

Thoughtless people will get out of this by saying: "I have not had a chance"; others, those whose thoughts are directed by a master mind, which is an adept at concentration, will recollect themselves, will mentally review all the passing events of the day, and will thereby, conclude that they are responsible for that happening so deplorable for their interest.

What then should they do?

Simply devote themselves to one of the exercises most recommended by thinkers; concentrate their faculties on the principal act of the day, which was the settlement of the business which called them out, and, once well persuaded of its importance, suit all their acts to it.

They would thus have avoided losing the few minutes or the hour which caused them to fail, for, filled with their determination, they would have cut short any business that it was not indispensable to conclude, or cut off some moments from talk the continuance of which was less important for them than the journey which they had to make.

"Each day," said Yoritomo, "brings with it a round of duties of unequal importance; we must know how to distinguish that which should take precedence, and subordinate to it, our mode of life for that day."

"Everything that we do should bear a relation to it; even if certain things should seem mutually exclusive, we must not avoid them, in as much as they form part of the whole of those things which go to make up realization."

"By being willing to sacrifice nothing, we succeed too often in accomplishing nothing."

"We know the story of the man who one day found two robbers in his garden and set out to pursue them."

"He ran after them at first for a time, then at a fork of the road, one of the two turned off to the right, while the other pursued his way."

"The man, undecided for a moment, rushed down the byroad, saying to himself that he would catch more easily the one that took the hard road, but after a time, out of breath, he perceived that he was not as quick as the robber, and bethought himself that the other was bigger and stouter and on that account easier to overtake."

"He, therefore, retraced his steps and rushed along the main road; but the man whom he was pursuing had

had the time, in spite of his want of agility, to gain ground, and the pursuer puffed and blew in vain. He soon had the mortification of seeing him disappear, and his neighbors made fun of him."

How many times do we act likewise, without perceiving it, when we pursue two different ends and give them up, first one, then the other, according to the inclination of our idleness or of our whims?

Those who practice concentration will never commit this fault. They will never risk making themselves a laughing-stock like the people of whom Yoritomo speaks, for they will set out in pursuit of an undertaking only after reflecting deeply on the possibilities of success, and they will take every precaution against giving it up before they have brought it to a successful issue.

They, who would be adequately prepared for this kind of reflection, ought to bring themselves to it by the habitual contemplation of a thought. Our thoughts are tools, and the life substance is shaped with these tools. Every hour we can stand before our half-formed self and with tools a thousand times finer than those of the finest craftsman of the physical plane, we can cut, from our own thought atmosphere, forms of exquisite perfection, until body, environment, friends, even our whole life, is a world picture of peace, power, love, joy, health and wealth, limitless and perfect.

It is well to maintain the attention on the alert, and to keep oneself from every distraction by the repetition of one or several sayings bearing a relation to this thought, giving it concrete and definite form and persuading ourselves of the necessity of concentration.

Other methods also, are employed with success; they make up those exercises that should be practiced by all those who wish to acquire any science, whatever it may be.

Of these methods, several were already known in the time of Yoritomo, and it is he who recommends us a procedure which he called "of the collar":

"Have," said he, "a collar containing about 200 beads of jade or of any other stone, if your means do not allow you to make use of jewels. Take care to string them, not too close together, in order to be able to take them off easily and make them slide slowly one over the other, counting ten between each bead."

"Your mind, during this time, should be occupied with only one thing: to allow between the beads the same space of time. Do not say the numbers too fast or too slowly, and do it in such a way, all the time, that this exercise lasts, as to think thus, regularly of nothing but GOOD."

"When you find it impossible to keep up your thought, revive it as soon as you can and begin again."

"At first, it will be well not to extend the experiment farther than five or six beads."

"Afterward you can increase it, and some thinkers are mentioned who had such a mastery over their imaginations, that they went right to the end of the beads without slackening."

With the same collar the Shogun shows us yet another exercise.

"You will take off," said he, "a handful of the beads (without counting them), in such a way that you are ignorant of the exact number, and, having fastened the collar together again, letting the place of joining be in sight, which will serve you as a starting-point, you will count aloud each bead that you take off with your finger-tip."

"That done, you will begin again three times - if you find the same number each time it means that your power of concentration has been sufficient to keep your attention without letting it wander."

"Where you find a different number, you should begin again until you obtain the same result three times in succession."

We might smile at the simplicity of these methods, nevertheless, those who are devoted adepts in concentration, know how difficult these results are to realize, if they wish to be sincere with themselves; before obtaining the same count of beads three times, they must often begin the experiment over again twenty times, for thought escapes easily when one can no longer keep it in subjection."

The Shogun recommends us yet other exercises:

"Sit down," said he, "comfortably on a seat, soft enough to prevent your feeling any discomfort; this is very essential, for the least physical discomfort distracts the attention by directing it to the feeling of uneasiness which you experience."

"That done you will rest your hands on your breast, the palms well open, the fingers spread out."

"The left hand will be placed near the waist and the other near the throat; you will slowly pass the left hand down to the waist, while you lift the other as far as the neck, taking great care, when the two hands meet, to touch lightly the tip of the middle finger of the left hand with the tip of the middle finger of the right hand."

"During the few minutes that this exercise lasts, you will do it in such a way as to think of nothing except the care of letting the fingers touch one another toward the middle of the breast, and in consequence, of accelerating or retarding the movement in order to arrive at this result."

"During all this time, force yourself to think of nothing else."

This is what our modern philosophers recommend under the name of "devitalization."

Devitalization is the act of shutting oneself out from external impressions and moral sensations; it is a kind of arrest of thought, or rather of rupture of thought, which one concentrates on something so plainly commonplace, that it gives birth to a sensible rest for us.

This is the first step, which leads to one of the most satisfactory forms of concentration - isolation.

Without isolation, no meditation is possible, and

consequently, there is great difficulty in concentration.

Now we have just seen, what part, this faculty plays in training the mind.

It is that which allows us to rally our scattered psychical powers and to unite them on the same point, localizing them alone on the phases of the subject that engages our attention.

It is also recommended that we devote ourselves to the study of any object, whatsoever, and force ourselves to limit the effort of our thoughts to that object alone.

But this meditation may form the excuse for many mental vagaries.

One way of accomplishing this is to take a piece of paper and to concentrate our attention solely on the thought of this scrap; but is not this, on the other hand, a dangerous excuse for fancy to come into play?

Contemplate it: this piece of paper once formed part of some material. What material? Was it the white muslin of bridal veils? Was it, on the other hand, the flimsy fabric in which a courtesan arrays herself? Whose hands tore it? In what religious processions or in what wretched dens was it used?

Later, by what changes did it come to this condition of a scrap of paper?

Doubtless, Yoritomo also believes this when he says:

"If you wish to devote yourself sincerely to the practice of concentration, guard yourself against allowing your thoughts to wander from the corolla to the stalk of the flower."

This means that one object alone, and that strictly limited, should engage our attention, if we wish to succeed in controlling our attention to the point at which it responds to our first call like an obedient servant.

Many feather-brained people think it a good excuse when they say:

"It is not my fault, I forgot."

Not suspecting that forgetfulness is itself the fault with which they do not wish to be charged. It is an excuse, glibly assigned by those, whose moral infirmity is so evident that they are unable, on their own account, to make any effort worth the while.

It is the excuse of the weak and of people lacking courage.

It is a certificate of psychical incapacity awarded to those who have not in them, the energy to practice self-recollection.

Meditation, which is closely allied to concentration, is a state of inward contemplation that allows us to shut ourselves in from external things, so as to engage our thoughts, solely on the subject that we have set before ourselves.

Many people over the centuries have practiced concentration by means of meditation. Some experts on meditation recommend that, to concentrate, one should focus one's mind on a mantra, a sound that they will repeat over and over again during their period of meditation. Preferably, it should be a sound that has no literal meaning, such as the humming sound "ommmmm". By repeating this mantra over and over, the mind is released from all other thoughts and it can concentrate on becoming totally relaxed.

Meditation gurus like the Maharishi Mahesh Yogi, who advocated the practice of transcendental meditation, a movement that became very popular in the mid-twentieth century, would personally give each of his followers their own mantra, a Sanskrit word that he felt fit that disciple's personality.

Some people prefer using a word or phrase that has special meaning for them. It may be a biblical text such as a brief proverb or part of a prayer. Some Catholics recite Ave Maria - some the entire prayer, some just the two-word title. Some select a specific thought that sets the stage for them. One woman reported that by just saying over and over Today is the day, she reinforced the principle that "yesterday is past and gone, tomorrow has not come, it is today that I must live now."

Select a mantra that best suits you. Incorporate this into your breathing exercises. Breathe in, repeat the mantra, as you breathe out over and over again.

The difference between meditation and concentration lies in the greater freedom allowed to thought in the former state.

"Meditation," said Yoritomo, "is like a target of which concentration is the bull's-eye."

"Every arrow which hits the target has certainly attained its end, but those which quiver at it center are the only ones which, in ease of defense, would have sufficed to make our enemy bite the dust."

And he adds:

"Meditation is valuable above all because it is a rest; it is a kind of mental anesthesia which allows us to have faith in our liberty of thought, even when, nevertheless, we still confine it but less closely than in concentration."

"We could not devote ourselves to a fruitful meditation without being prepared for it by self-absorption."

"We must then allow ourselves to be slowly permeated by the idea which we wish to fathom and all the influences of which we wish to receive."

"But we ought to fear one redoubtable enemy - distraction. Nothing is more difficult for those, who do not habitually practice this lesson, than to meditate successfully, without letting the thoughts wander after ideas which are connected with one another, but which end by reason of their number and diversity, by being completely removed from the initial point."

In fact, we have all experienced the impression of which the Shogun speaks; it has happened to all of us, after long periods of reflection, to find ourselves a hundred miles from the subject which we desired to conjure up, and when we wish to take account of the road traversed, we find ourselves altogether amazed at the imperceptible concatenation of thoughts, which, without seeming to be foreign to the subject of our meditation, have drawn us in the direction of ideas completely dissimilar.

This is one of the familiar phases of distraction, that foe of concentration.

This is why Yoritomo puts us on our guard against pseudo-meditation, of which day-dreaming is, he says, the mischievous sister.

"Let us beware," says he, "of allowing ourselves to give way to day-dreaming, for thus we should contract the undesirable habit of allowing our attention to drowse; day-dreaming is a fabric on which fancy embroiders shapeless flowers, it scatters them without method or system at its own sweet will; these flowers are unreal and their colors soon fade."

"Day-dreaming is a dissipation of energy, it carries us away and we cannot direct it."

"For this reason it is particularly dangerous, for it destroys our psychic forces and injures the development of strong mental powers."

It was with this in view, it is said, that a twelfth century Castillian friar, St. Dominic, invented the rosary.

He thought, like our Japanese philosopher, that meditation is so close akin to daydreaming, that one should seek to control it by removing the temptations arising from the volatility of the imagination by means of a physical rallying of the idea.

The telling of the beads has no other object; all the decades end in a different prayer from the ten preceding it and, granting that the attention has wandered during the repetition of the ten "Hail Marys," the eleventh bead, separate from the others and appreciatively larger, comes to remind us of the change of the formula and brings back the most wandering minds to the subject of the meditation.

In short, such a director of souls as St. Dominic, knew well that day-dreaming always possesses a pernicious charm which it is well to nip in the bud.

A great thinker, the eighteenth century French philosopher, Etienne Condillac, said further:

"Attention is like a light which is reflected from one body onto another, in order to illuminate both of them, and I call it reflection."

"...Sensible ideas represent to us the objects which actually impress themselves on our senses; intellectual ideas represent to us those which disappear after making their impression..."

He also said:

"Intellectual ideas, if they are familiar to us, recur to us at will."

This was also the teaching of Yoritomo, who wrote:

"It suffices for those who practice concentration, to will for the objects on which they wish to meditate, to be recalled clearly before their eyes."

"Adepts in this art can, with very little effort and after placing themselves in a condition of self-absorption, transport themselves in imagination to the sphere where the phases of the occurrence which forms the subject of their thought unfold themselves before them."

"They will succeed in picturing to themselves places and persons in living movement, in so realistic a manner that they will even be sensible of the odors or the climate of the place that witnesses these happenings."

"What marvel that, finding themselves in this mental condition, it is easy for them to decide on sound resolutions and to thrust aside attempts to counsel for them a less studied decision?"

And he concludes:

"Those who would influence others should, above all things, know how to influence themselves in order to acquire the faculty of self-concentration which will allow, of their reaching, the highest degree of discernment."

Many soothsayers have owed their influence over the multitude only to that spirit of concentrations that passed for prophecies.

"It is wrong and delusive to give credence to magic, which is trickery, but we bear within us a power equal to that of the sorcerers whose deeds are related; this is the magic of the influence which prudent and self-possessed people always exercise over others , when their intentions are pure and when their ideals are nothing else than the amelioration of the condition of others, by the wholesome influence of their example and discourse."

LESSON XI

By Confidence

Confidence is the mental impulse that all those who wish to influence others should seek to elicit.

For most of them, it is the means of replacing the vacillating and ever faltering will with their own will, which they impose according to circumstances and according to the character of their followers.

With some, gentle persuasion is a means, even if slow, yet almost sure of success.

But we must guard the future adept from a diversity of influences, otherwise our minds will always retain the most recent impression, and before following the course of initiation, we must give our attention to doing away with contradictory ideas that we cannot completely eradicate, except with great difficulty.

This is one of the characteristics of feeble folk; their stubbornness has always to be cornbatted and we cannot succeed in teaching them confidence, except after prolonged effort.

The best way left to us is not to hit them too hard, for their obstinacy - which they sometimes take for will-power - would form a troublesome obstacle to their conversion.

It is, therefore, better to seem to pay attention to their opinions, however baseless they may be, and to put before them objections, that appear rather involuntary, than otherwise and which to all appearances we regret the necessity of formulating.

This is what Yoritomo teaches us in the following anecdote:

"My-master Lang-Ho," said he, "had among his disciples, a chief, who had great influence in the senate, not on account of his personal qualifications, but rather of his wealth which was considerable."

"He had estates the extent of which gave him the privileges of a little king, and my master thought rightly, that such a man should be gained over, to the beauty of the Good, in order that his discourse should not be like the weeds of the field, but on the contrary, should resemble good seed, the sprouting of which brings forth a whole course of bountiful harvest."

"But this nobleman suffered from a weakness of will that hindered him from profiting by any lesson."

"He would say 'yes' one day and the next day, after listening to the talk of those, who had no other idea except to get money out of him, he would profess an opposite opinion and set himself obstinately to follow the most pernicious counsels."

"Lang-Ho, as I have already told you, was a profound psychologist; no recess of the human heart was hidden from him; so, after subjecting the chief to a lengthy scrutiny, he adopted the method which seemed likely to succeed."

"He did not dissuade him from acts, which under evil influences, this man had made up his mind to perform, but at first he, so to speak, channeled his infatuation toward things of less importance, the plan of which he seemed at first to entertain kindly."

"He was careful thus not to awaken the spirit of obstinacy which he knew was dormant in the chief's heart. But after putting him to the test and at the time when the latter was no longer in a suspicious mood, Lang-Ho enumerated to him the errors of his ways and did not fail to declare what mischief would accrue from them."

"This done, he let him follow his own devices or rather those of his evil counselors."

"This policy had the result of allowing the troubles which he had foretold to arise, so that by degrees the chief began to regard Lang-Ho with a kind of superstitious fear, blended with a deep veneration."

"The philosopher waited no longer; he then took in hand the freeing of his disciple from his self-interested friends, and after some months of initiation, the latter, imbued with the knowledge and wisdom of the master, ceased all resistance and gloried in showing to those who depended on him that he shared the opinions of the sage."

"From that to conversion, was only one step, and that step was taken so successfully that, under the influence of Lang-Ho, the chief became a genuine benefactor to all who lived on his estates and who looked up to him as a master whose word has the force of an oracle."

But certain natures are restive under persuasion or two, malleable for any impression to leave its marks on them.

In such, therefore, it is well to inspire confidence, somewhat in spite of themselves, by having recourse to suggestion.

All modern thinkers are of this opinion, all those also who are engaged with mental infirmities:

We too readily give an idea of magic to the word suggestion.

Suggestion, as the writer understands it, might be defined as follows:

The development of confidence.

It is, in a way, the imposing of one's belief on the mind of others; it is not a quack method of enthralling people and of compelling them to carry out tasks which we feel ourselves but do not have the courage to perform; it is a noble faculty which choice spirits alone possess, that of implanting their belief in those whom they consider worthy of being persuaded.

Be it remembered that there is suggestion in everything; in the book which fascinates us and the theories of which gain possession of us in spite of ourselves; in the conversation to which we listen of our own accord, in the discussions of which only one side seems to us to express the truth.

But it happens, too frequently, that if afterwards we recollect ourselves in order to judge our thoughts with the same impartiality, as we should those of others, we are, altogether, amazed to see the fine enthusiasm that had animated us, fail; the principles of the book, stripped of the magic of style, seem to us highly debatable; the conversation which we enjoyed, when the illusion of eloquence no longer illumines it, seems to us insipid, and the object of discussion, which had interested us deeply, becomes a matter of indifference to us, when we examine it calmly.

To what then is this sudden change to be ascribed?

Does it arise from ourselves? From our over-susceptibility to enthusiasm, or from our excessive propensity to fleeting impressions?

In most cases regarding these suggestions we should accuse only their authors, who, not being convinced themselves, have been unable to imbue us with a lasting confidence.

To inspire confidence without which no influence is possible, several qualities are indispensable:

- Sincerity with ourselves.
- Hatred of injustice;
- Certainty in our decisions;
- Absolute truth in our predictions;
- Confidence in our own merits.

Sincerity with ourselves consists, especially, in the conviction of the necessity that exists of making others share in a belief, the good effects of which we experience so deeply, that the failure to diffuse it abroad should seem to us a dereliction of all our duties.

You see why the appeal of missionaries is generally so powerful; the success of the apostolate is always subordinated to the sincerity of the convictions of those who expound them and to their certainty that they are performing a duty in inculcating them on those for whom they may prove a support and a consolation.

If speakers doubt their own statements, their voices will be less firm, the effulgence of their thoughts will less easily spread over the audience, and enthusiasm, the parent of absolute faith, will not lift them to carry them on their way.

But how different a reception will be accorded to the apostles who are themselves convinced. Let us listen to Yoritomo in this matter:

"Like a refreshing stream," said he, "the words of those who believe spread into the minds of their hearers and quench their thirst of moral support and lofty convictions."

"Like moths attracted by the light of tapers, they will all flock around those who are for them the light and know how to envelop them with its life-giving rays."

"As long as they speak, vistas of brightness are spread before them; if they vanish, they seem again to pass into darkness, only brightened by the remembrance of the words of confidence and faith."

Those who know not hatred of injustice will never be able to exercise a salutary influence on others.

How could they attract to themselves confidence, the mother of conversion, if, by the unfairness of their judgments, they are subjected to that of others?

"No partiality," said Yoritomo, "should animate those who would win souls."

It is by allowing themselves to fall into such lapses that they will lose all the authority which they would fain acquire.

"Strict justice alone should direct their words and preside over their acts."

"Where they are themselves quite in the dark and do not see on which side justice is ranged, they should refrain, until the time, when a close concentration permits them to see the situation clearly."

"If doubt continues, let them be very careful not to utter a decision, the injustice of which, events might demonstrate, thus weakening the trust which their disciples are pleased to place in them."

"It is more honorable to confess one's ignorance than to risk committing an injustice."

To secure certainty in our judgments, it is prudent sometimes to use artifice, like the sage of whose shrewdness Yoritomo tells us.

"It should never happen," said he, "that those who wish to inspire confidence should risk seeing it destroyed by an assertion that is not borne out by facts."

"In this matter, it is wise to imitate the old philosopher Hong-Yi who would never say, 'That will happen,' but, 'you have acted in such a way as to bring on yourself such or such a misfortune,' or, 'you are acting with so much prudence as to deserve to be rewarded.' "

"So that when events happened to confirm his learned forecasts, he did not fail to recall his sayings and his authority, thereby, increased more and more."

"It should be added that the events foreseen, always came to pass, for the deductive powers of Hong-Yi were great and it was easy for him to presume the acts which his disciples might be expected to perform!"

But foreseeing and even prophesying are not sufficient to gain confidence, and especially, to communicate it.

In order to implant it in the hearts of others, it is necessary to possess it - this splendid confidence in ourselves that works wonders.

Then, it is that all those to whom thinking for themselves is a labor, those whose powers of resistance are fitful and ill-balanced, those whose moral idleness rises up against all individual initiative, will lift their heads and feel a new strength, relying on the feeling of confidence, which they will experience, first in the master and afterward in themselves.

The healing balm of faith will, by its good qualities,

impregnate them in the gentlest fashion and, despising the faintheartedness that hitherto had marked their most trivial resolutions, they will advance fearlessly toward the goal that has become plainly visible to their sight.

It is a well-known fact that an imagined support often serves as well as the support itself.

We know the instance of toddlers who cannot bring themselves to walk without stumbling but who, as soon as we stretch out a finger to them, pretending thus to support them, steadies their steps in such a way, that they can accomplish a walk of several yards without tottering.

If, however, we draw back the finger, which, as it seems to them, is the support that must guard them from falling, they advance a few steps with difficulty and cannot avoid tumbling down.

It is the same with timid souls; people who think they will die of fear in the solitude of an empty house will, feel quite reassured if they imagine that the adjacent rooms are occupied.

The presence of others, creating a feeling of confidence in possible protection, suffices to save them from the fear, which they would not fail to experience, if they thought that, in case of need, there was no one to help them.

This protection, even when they know it to be illusory, suffices to allay their apprehensions.

Thus, although they are quite sure that they can expect nothing from the intervention of a child; timid persons almost always seek such company rather than remain alone, and they experience from it a real relief.

"Every impression," says Yoritomo, "which is not our own and which comes from outside is an influence which we perforce put up with."

"It is especially in cases of sickness that this influence can make its presence felt in the highest degree, for at such a time, the subjects being very weak, is best disposed to submit themselves to any suggestion whatsoever."

"There is a vague solidarity between mind and body which allows of the latter becoming as easy prey to affective conditions brought about by suffering."

"It would be idle to deny the connection between our physical ills and our mental sufferings."

"Some under the domination of weighty anxieties, become the victims of severe headache."

"Others again, after repeated emotional disturbances, contract heart troubles."

"It is, therefore, sometimes wiser to cure the mind before considering how to care for the body, or rather it is well to effect both cures at the same time."

"Now it is that influence makes itself felt, triumphant, radiant; it stamps on the nerve centers, an impression, which reverberates through one's whole being."

"Considering that our troubles are due to pain, to anxiety, to hypochondria, we should cultivate confidence and cheerfulness which take from our conceptions their somber coloring."

"If we have been able to inspire invalids with confidence, we shall be glad to tell them that they are getting better, for they will not doubt the truth of the assertion and that assurance will cause them to experience a real improvement."

"Miracles have no other basis than this."

And the Shogun proceeds:

"But the grandest means of effecting these cures is to implant in the mind of self-imagined invalids the idea of devotion to a noble cause; to plunge them into a tide of ambition that will make them gradually forget their everlasting 'Ego.' For this over-coddled 'Ego' is the real cause of most of these disorders from which all persons suffer whom a surfeit of 'Ego' so dominates that their most trivial ailments command their whole attention and seem to them to be entitled to command that of everybody else to the exclusion of all other things."

"On such, influence should be exercised in quite different a manner."

"It will suffice to create about them an atmosphere of activity in which their personality will play a dominating part; they will thus, forget to spend their time in looking out for the attacks of an illness which exists only in their own brain, and those who assists them to a cure may congratulate themselves doubly, for they will have made their beneficial influence felt in the case of both mind and body."

"Assuredly, the best of suggestions is that which lies in, as it were, devitalizing the self-centered person, by substituting for the worshiper of his or her 'Ego' an altruist who, thoroughly imbued with faith in him or herself and strong in the mission with which that person truly believes, will seek to impart to others the benefits of that confidence from which that person has derived so much consolation."

Thus, will the advice of Yoritomo be proved right when he says:

"Let those who feel themselves to be in the right and have Confidence in themselves, rise up and proclaim this faith, so that the weak, the vacillating, and all those who suffer from doubt may flock around them to warm themselves at the genial blaze that issues from the fire of contentment of which their minds are full."

LESSON XII

Acquisition of Dominating Power

"The warriors of old," said Yoritomo, "were very fond of insignia, which they believed to be likely to impress their enemies."

"They liked to wear fearsome masks, the manes of beasts, or helmets the top of which represented the head of an animal."

"One great general arrayed himself in a helmet, the tip of which bore the figure of a mattock (a digging tool in which the blade is perpendicular to the handle - used as a combined pick and shovel) and on the visor were engraven characters, the combination of which represented the words 'mattock', 'way', and 'rock', which the learned have interpreted as follows:

"If the 'way' is not opened by my 'mattock', I will lay it out even in the 'rock.' "

"Now what idea dominated all those warriors if not the desire to impress their enemies, some by fear, others by intimidation?"

"But there is a kind of influence - a thousand fold more valuable than all these rude methods and barbarous attempts to bring about an emotion by means of bloodthirsty symbols."

"The domain of thought is open to all those who feel themselves worthy of entering it; it is for those who know the turnings of a beautiful garden with multifarious paths."

"On each fresh excursion, they discover some hitherto unknown paths which they explore always with increasing interest."

"The flowers which border them are gorgeous or poor, according as they shed on them, the rays of intelligence placed at the disposal of the powers of the will which are latent in them."

"But those whose languid action can not lift the torch, whose indolence neglects to enkindle, do not enjoy the sight of these diversified flowers."

"In the gloom from which they look on them, they perceive them but indistinctly, and the path seems to them so uninteresting that they lose the desire to seek in it for new objects."

"Those, on the other hand, who know how to throw the floral beauties into the light derive from their contemplation so exquisite an enjoyment, that there always arises in them, the desire for fresh explorations, and also the wish to share their admiration, by introducing some persons to the marvels which they have encountered, and by teaching others how to see them in all their splendor."

"This is the secret of the dominating influence which certain people exercise over others."

"Those alone who know how to throw the flowers of thought into the light, after having sought and found them, can acquire sufficient power to influence the destinies of others."

This is what, in language less florid but nonetheless ornate, modern thinkers tell us:

There is an intercommunication between ourselves and others of such a nature that perpetually, night and day, we are receiving and giving forth again influences which model us, change us, and gradually alter our mode of life.

It is, therefore, through instigation for without that we end by making ourselves what we are: good or bad, happy or miserable.

Thought plays a decisive part in human life. It encompasses the individual. It is the cord which binds us to others and by means of which are gathered together, to join and mingle in a single current, all surrounding energies."

It is a method of acquiring the power necessary to first subdue those whom we wish afterward to influence:

"By causing mental currents to pass from you to the other parties under the form of timely questions and suggestions, you awaken in them responsive currents; you find out their likes and dislikes, and, by encouraging their confidence, through the current derived from an approval delicately expressed, you will soon succeed in making them vibrate in unison with yourself."

Those who would acquire the power of domination over the minds of those they wish to direct must, above all, compel themselves to create between them and their disciple, a kind of intellectual level which will be of infinite service to those people.

It is by creating empathy that these vibrations in unison, so indispensable in the formation of influence, will be obtained.

Empathy - the art of truly understanding another by "putting oneself in that person's shoes" - begets confidence and paves the way for beneficent suggestion.

"Those who know how to attract empathy," said Yoritomo, " is like a kindly light toward which turn all those whose minds are covered with moral darkness."

"Their development is rarely very speedy, and that is preferable, otherwise they would be dazzled before being enlightened; it is better to attract them slowly but irresistibly."

"Then, already imbued with the distant radiance, they will already have come out of darkness when they approach quite near to those who are to give them clear light and, grown familiar with the brilliant rays, they will endure its utmost intensity without flinching."

It is, in fact, one of the powers of empathy to attract slowly but to retain surely those who feel themselves drawn to an empathetic-person by an attraction at first vague and ill-defined, later justified by a thousand reasons, the principal of which, and soon the only one, will be the attraction which those, who possess dominating power, exert over others.

It is better, as Yoritomo says, for this power to assert itself less, roughly to have more chances of permanency.

It is preferable to illumine slowly, people's minds, with a well-defined gleam than to dazzle them to the extent of causing them a discomfort, which will make them seek the darkness as a relief.

One of the secrets of dominating power lies in exciting similarity of feelings by adopting for the time being those, which are within the compass of those whom we wish to influence.

The feeling of condescension should be given up by strong minds. Those who believe that they are lowering themselves with regard to their disciples, by instilling in them principles which they regard as too elementary, will never succeed as a leader.

Those who would use the power of suggestion in earnest should for a moment give up their own minds to adopt that of the persons they are teaching. This is the only way of creating a bond of mutual confidence.

"Those who would teach the first characters in writing should be able to create a child's mind in themselves," said the Shogun.

We must admit that, to fulfill this condition, it is necessary to be already in possession of a rare self-mastery.

Only those who can master themselves are qualified to master others.

If ambition and confidence in one's own worth are the attributes of dominating power, self-sufficiency is always the stumbling block over which one trips for pride prevents from looking down at one's own feet.

Self-sufficiency almost always begets arrogance, which is of no use for producing empathy and confidence.

This exaggerated idea of "Ego" is never dictated by the consciousness of real merit, but rather by the imaginary swelling of virtues that we ascribe too freely to ourselves, as though to divert our minds with the noise of our own words.

If we wish to be sincere, we shall recognize very quickly that these virtues are imaginary, and that the parade that we make of them arises only from a great desire to possess them; but, the power having failed for assuring the gaining of them, we prefer, by proclaiming loudly that we possess them, to shirk the effort of acquiring them.

This is why egotistical, smug persons, in the category of whom we must place those out of whom an empty pride beats out nobility of character, will never have the aptitude for exerting an influence over the minds of others.

Unable to derive from themselves, the energy necessary to become what they would like to be, they cannot emit around themselves that power which fails them, and their domination over others will never be established.

Melancholy persons, those who are the victims of hypochondria, are by no means destined to become shepherds of the multitude.

Melancholy almost always begets a mental condition bordering on indifference; it suppresses the desire for life, the key of all good resolutions and continual perseverance.

Every effort of the melancholy is quickly halted by that terrible thought, "What is the good?" which proclaims the end of everything and the vanity of life.

What influence can people exercise if their powers of energy are destroyed by indifference and apathy?

They have hardly the strength to live themselves; where will they find the strength to teach others?

Cheerfulness is one of the requisite conditions for controlling others; not that boisterous mirth which is made up of bursts of laughter, the reasons for which are not always of the most refined nature, but that inward peace which we define as cheerfulness and which is the mark of highly developed minds.

People of fine character will never be melancholy. Hypochondria is the trade-mark of the incapable; it is the commencement of manias and of all crazes that desolate humanity and abase its moral level.

The philosophers of ill-omen, whose teaching has clouded so many young brains, have defined enjoyment as follows: "Cessation of suffering."

Ah, well! But is not that worth an effort, to suffer no longer, and can we regard as a madman, the people who labor to end this suffering, by substituting for it the joy of living, which opens minds to the cult of beauty?

The art of happiness lies especially in the great wish to live.

If Yoritomo was not willing to raise the burning question of free will, he nonetheless admits the unquestionable influence of each one of us on our own destiny.

"We," said he, "are for the most part like the fool who shivered, cowering in a snowdrift, while around him the sun bathed the mountain with its burning rays."

"He cursed the snow, the cold, the hateful country where he dwelt, and the misery of his existence which had to be spent in suffering and barrenness."

"In vain, people signaled to him of nearby paths, in vain they showed him, from afar, flowers gathered on the way; he was obstinately bent on doing nothing to free himself from his sufferings and continued to curse the place which it would have been so easy to leave and deplored the unhappiness of the fate which had caused him to be born in that inclement country."

Have we not here, in very truth, the picture of the pessimist who denies the existence of happiness and beauty while pretending to turn away when they pass?

Such persons may perchance exercise a pernicious influence over weak minds, but it will always be limited, for we cannot repeat it too often - real influence over others is only acquired at the price of complete mastery of oneself.

This mastery should be the aim of the efforts of those who wish to possess this faculty and to make use of it for their own happiness and that of those with whom they come in contact.

"Again," said the Nippon philosopher, "we should keep ourselves from too commonplace associations, for, granting this truth that the thought which we emit about us is taken in by those around, we ought to beware of the imbibing of commonplace thought which, when repeated too often, will end by occupying, unknown to ourselves, a place in our brain and will weaken the quality of the power."

"The higher type person should never harbor a medley of ideas."

"Those who frame, the waves of which spread themselves around them, succeed by a succession of undulating movements which may be compared with those of sound, in striking the intelligence of others by setting their brains in vibration, in other words, in a state to receive the floating thought."

"But the really forceful people, those whose secret energies are concentrated on the gaining of influence, those who aim to acquire dominating power, will harbor no ignoble thoughts, for they will not barter away the first to arrive of these flowers of the mind; if they find themselves among people of small intellectual caliber, they will surpass them with all the mighty power that their knowledge and strength of will confer.

"They will know how to listen to other people, then to talk to them, perhaps to convince them, but not for a moment will they submit themselves to imbibing their commonplace thoughts. For having come among them in as apostles they are conscious of their own excellence. They know too well their own superiority. They are, in a word, on too lofty a pedestal, to allow themselves to be affected by things beneath them.

"Does the granite stoop to the ivy that twines itself about it while mounting toward the towers in its need of protection and support?"

The Shogun remarks also that this plant, which, without the support of the granite, would trail miserably on the ground, ends, when it has covered the surface at every point, by forming an essential part of the building, to such a degree that its frail tendrils effect more for the durability of the works of man than the hardest marbles chiseled by the most skilful artisans.

And he adds:

"How many ancient towers, that seemed of unquestionable solidity, crumble to pieces when deprived of the parasites that seemed to overrun them?"

"So it is with all those who possess power; they maintain themselves only because they create disciples whose devotion serves to consolidate their work."

"But if they cannot retain the influence, which at first they had sent forth around them, their followers fall away one by one, and they, left alone, soon see the edifice of their superiority crumble to pieces."

"Dominating power," Yoritomo proceeds, "is developed especially by an apostolate the exercise of which, by creating a mental current between the masters and those whom they are teaching, wards off opposing currents."

In the cant of modern science it is said in fact that material builders, drawn by the attractive force of thought, are always displaced in feeble minds by a stronger influence, bit that the converse does not hold good.

Such is the comment of the Japanese philosopher when he tells us:

"Do not rub shoulders with a commonplace mind except with the intention of raising that person to your own level, but do not think of entering in mental communion with such before making it worthy of it."